Handbook for HOT WITCHES

Handbook

for

HOT
WITCHES

Dame Darcy

Henry Holt and Company
New York

Any reader who uses the spells in this book does so at her own risk, and the author and publisher accept no liability if the spells do not have the desired effect.

Photo credits for hot witch friends on pp. 192–93 are courtesy of the following: Billy & Hells (Jessie Evans); E. Bruce Stanger (Angela Devine); Alia Penner (Miss KK); Star Foreman (Batcakes); Doug Jaeger (Jessica Delfino); Ben Cain (Kai Altair); Robert Costello (Ophelia DeLaFuente); Steven Rosen (Shien Lee); Steve Leialoha (Trina Robbins); Mark Brady (Rachel Amodeo).

Henry Holt and Company, LLC, *Publishers since 1866*
175 Fifth Avenue, New York, New York 10010
macteenbooks.com

Henry Holt® is a registered trademark of Henry Holt and Company, LLC.
Copyright © 2012 by Dame Darcy
All rights reserved.

Library of Congress Cataloging-in-Publication Data
Darcy, Dame.
Handbook for hot witches / Dame Darcy. — 1st ed.
p.   cm.
ISBN 978-0-8050-9379-7
1. Witchcraft. 2. Teenagers. I. Title. BF1571.5.T44D37 2012 133.4'3—dc23 2011041297

First Edition—2012 / Designed by April Ward
Printed in the United States of America

1 3 5 7 9 10 8 6 4 2

✦✶† Contents †✶✦

✦✶✦ Introduction ✦✶✦
What's a Hot Witch?

A witch is someone who is blessed with extra abilities. Being in touch with your *sense* of intuition or compassion, or being able to *see* things others can't or create things others don't dream of—these are all powerful abilities.

What makes you different from everybody else? Some people can recognize that you have something special and will call this *weird*, which is a word often used to describe witches in old stories. The witches in Shakespeare's *Macbeth*, for instance, are Weird Sisters.

To some people being weird and talented is amazing, and they love you even more for it. They recognize the importance of diversity in every circle of life, and they celebrate differences, knowing that they make a stronger whole.

But there are some who just want to fit in and be like everyone else. This is a losing game—ultimately everyone is different and, thus, "weird." These are the people who changed *witch* into a negative word and used it to single out and condemn people (especially girls) who have exceptional qualities.

I personally take back the term *witch* and the power that belongs to it, and I make it my own so that if anyone ever calls me weird, it is a compliment and not an insult.

Witches go back to the time of the bards, who were the first storytellers. Because no mail service, Internet, or newspapers existed then, bards traveled from one town to another recounting stories and news. Often these tales were in rhyme and song, because when words rhyme, they are easier to remember. This is also why spells, chants, and mantras often rhyme.

Bards were equally men and women. So if you were a girl then, and you didn't want to play the traditional role of farmer's wife, you were said to be "born to the bard," and this was a career option for you.

And there were other options for women as well. You could be an herbalist or a midwife, and treat people's illnesses. You could study nature and the stars as a physicist or an astronomer.

You could write poetry or play the harp; you could be a scribe, taking down notes and letters for important people. And you could become a priestess or a Druid, and lead festivals and guide people through their lives. These were all positions of power and prestige held by women in ancient times. These witches were considered exceptional. As most people did not have the skills to hold these jobs, a witch's place in society was honored and needed.

These girls were considered "hot" for being witches—they were cherished like precious gems, each for her original contribution to society and family. They were loved by the community and by guys who could see that what witches have is exceptional and sexy.

The skills these witches had are still needed today and hold an important role in our current time. Science, technology, biology, spirituality, academia, and the arts can all lend themselves to helping the environment and our society.

To be a hot witch is to understand and control your spirit, mind, and body; to know your talents and skills; and to identify your passion. We can revolutionize the world we were born into by using the witchcraft skills of compassion, genius, insight, intuition, and talent.

The time we live in now is a turning point: Society, nature, and the way we interact with each other are all changing. In this crucial time, we girls need to remember who we really are and to let out that hot witch!

Dame Darcy

QUIZ
Which Type of Hot Witch Are You?

Everyone has her own talents and strengths. This book will highlight a number of types of hot witches. Each section includes activities, advice, and spells that its type of hot witch might find interesting. Before you get started, find out which type you are!

You will probably be a mix of several of the witches profiled, so the quiz will help you decide who you are the most like, or what blend of types make up your personality.

Hot Witch # 1

A. I want to be a party planner, events coordinator, or music promoter. I also would love to do weddings.

Yes or No

B. When my friends have relationship problems, they come to me for advice.

Yes or No

C. I like to decorate and design—especially interior design.

Yes or No

D. My own fashion is better than anything I ever see in stores. It's superfun to go thrifting and to mix and match.

Yes or No

Answer: If you answered Yes to two or more questions . . .

It is likely you are a Hot Witch Enchantress. Everything turns glamorous when the bewitching, charming, fascinating Enchantress touches it. She brings the party with her wherever she goes, and she is a delight and pleasure to all. Her beauty and charisma are unparalleled.

Enchantress

Hot Witch #2

A. Traveling and exploring new places is a lifelong dream of mine.

Yes or No

B. I have a whole book of poems and songs I have written and know by heart, or I love to make up stories and write fairy tales.

Yes or No

C. I would like to be a journalist or on-site news reporter.

Yes or No

D. Being a rock star, playing instruments and singing, is my ideal way of life.

Yes or No

Answer: If you answered Yes to two or more questions . . .

It is likely you are a Hot Witch Bard. A Bard loves doing all sorts of creative things. You'll find her writing, crafting, or dancing until the sun comes up.

Bard

Hot Witch # 3

A.   I can see fairies!

Yes or *No*

B.   Planting a garden and making food from my harvest is the greatest reward on earth.

Yes or *No*

C.   We are all one.

Yes or *No*

D.   I am an environmentalist.

Yes or *No*

Answer: If you answered Yes to two or more questions . . .

It is likely you are a Hot Witch Pagan Priestess. A Pagan is someone in touch with nature, literally "rustic," or "of the country." Pagans believe that everything is interconnected, alive, and divine. Everything has its own spirit. "I salute the divinity in you" is a common Pagan greeting. Pagan Priestesses are champions of diversity, minimal ecological impact, liberty, positive action, responsibility, and equality.

Pagan

Hot Witch #4

A. I can remember my past life, and I was a witch then, too.

Yes or *No*

B. When I go to an antiques store, I can see the previous owners of the furniture sitting in the chairs.

Yes or *No*

C. To me a mirror is just another doorway.

Yes or *No*

D. No one can ever lie to me.

Yes or *No*

Answer: If you answered Yes to two or more questions . . .

It is likely you are a Hot Witch Mystic. Mystics are highly spiritual, profound people in touch with the magical world to the highest degree. Using her vast experience, a Mystic can see through anything to its core of truth, and she has very strong intuitive powers beyond rational explanation.

Mystic

Hot Witch #5

A. Tarot cards, tea leaves, and a crystal ball: with these I feel and can see all! Ha ha ha!

Yes or *No*

B. Shapes in the fire show another universe.

Yes or *No*

C. I know things without knowing how I learned them.

Yes or *No*

D. Everyone calls me an "old soul."

Yes or *No*

Answer: If you answered Yes to two or more questions . . .

It is likely you are a Hot Witch Seer. A Seer (also known as a Sybil or Oracle) uses her extraordinary moral and spiritual insight to predict things to come. Using magical techniques to practice divination, Seers can find information and see the future.

SEER

Now that you know what kind of hot witch(es) you
are, go look them up in the table of contents and
get started exploring your handbook!

Enchantress

E verything turns glamorous when the bewitching, charming, fascinating Enchantress touches it. She brings the party with her wherever she goes, and she is a delight and pleasure to all. Her beauty and charisma are unparalleled.

✦✧ How to Be an Enchantress in Love ✧✦

No one is going to lead you to true happiness except yourself. When you have fun and delight in being your own unique, adorable self, you will attract love naturally.

Be enthusiastic, but mysterious. Don't show him all your cards at once, but also, don't play games. Always tell the truth.

When a guy does something you like, acknowledge him (this is something that works with all people, no matter what their gender or how old they are).

Guys like to feel they are winning a challenge. If you back off so they can pursue you a little bit, they feel like they have won a prize when you finally do decide.

If you need advice about your boyfriends, talk to your girlfriends or your mom. Don't tell too many people. Keep it to just your best friends.

Guys are usually a little behind girls as far as matters of the heart and being civilized go. But that's not their fault. They're born that way, even the poetic and artistic ones. But just like you, they want compassion, understanding, and a chance to prove themselves. When a magical lady approves of and shows appreciation to a guy, he transforms from a feral animal into a prince!

Be confident. Men love to see women enjoy themselves, and for a man to be in the presence of a lady like that is irresistible—even if you do it quietly and subtly.

A guy wants to be the icing on your cake, not the whole cake itself. That's too much pressure, and too much cake! If he knows you have an elaborate, lovely cake of a life and he is just the manly frosting on top, then the pressure is off and he can have fun.

Dame Darcy

Maybe you think you are a weirdo and there are no guys for you, but in reality there are plenty to choose from if you are able to have fun wherever you are.

Make room in your life for a boyfriend, and one will manifest. While you wait for him to call, have fun with your life and fill it with friends. Granny always said, "A watched pot never boils." But she also said, "There's a lid for every pot."

Relationships are an opportunity and a privilege, not a right. You and he have equal responsibilities to make a relationship work, so if either of you is being a spoiled brat with an attitude of entitlement, knock it off, step back, and apologize.

If you don't like something, he's much more likely to hear you if you say it conversationally rather than screaming.

When a guy acts ignorant about girls, it's because he hasn't learned the truth yet. You can be the one who teaches him. And you can do it nicely.

What If I Don't Like Guys?

Being gay is as natural as being straight. In many cultures throughout history, it has been accepted as a viable way to be, and a ton of people today feel the same. If you question your sexuality and wonder if you may be a lesbian or bisexual, seek out friends or family that you trust to talk about it with. If you don't feel like you have anyone to talk to, go online and find communities in your area that can offer you advice, or seek a counselor. Don't take ignorant or hurtful comments to heart; many people say and do mean things to mask their own insecurities or avoid the questions they have about their own sexuality.

A Word About Soul Mates...

A soul mate is someone you have known and been intimately connected to in another life. You meet again in this lifetime to continue the connection you began in another time and place.

If you meet your soul mate, you will be drawn to him or her at the cost of everything else. You will recognize this person as someone it feels like you have known forever. It will be an undeniable and irreversible bond that will change your life. If you are ready for a love like this, then you are ready to meet your soul mate. If it works, you will have your ideal partner, and one of the most magical bonds known to humankind. However, relationships between soul mates can be challenging and do not always work out. A soul mate is a mirror, one that reflects many aspects of your true self— every horrid detail and every beautiful dream. If both people are not ready to really look at themselves, they may attack and abandon a soul mate because they cannot step up. I think of it like a cobra striking at its own reflection.

⁜✦ Love Spells ✦⁜

Spell to Heal a Broken Heart

When the moon is waning (decreasing in size), take a mirror and put it in the bottom of a bowl of water. Light four silver candles, place them around the bowl, and gaze into the water at your own reflection for as long as the candles are burning (or whatever is comfortable). As you do so, say, "Take this pain from me and make it fade, as shadows do at the light of day."

Imagine the old you of the reflection being absorbed into the water. Imagine your pain being absorbed as well. Put it all there and really feel it. If tears fall into the water, that's fine. Let it all out. When the candles have burned down, throw the water away in a river or stream. The water must be moving away from you. If there is no moving body of water nearby, throw it down the drain. Take the mirror, wrap it in white cloth, and keep it in a drawer or another dark place for a month.

Dame Darcy

Love Potion Number Nine

Combine one spoonful of each of these seven types of leaves: rosehip, hibiscus, ginger, peppermint, lemon, red raspberry, and spice.

Boil water and pour it into a teapot. Place your blended tea into a tea ball and steep in the pot. Add lavender honey and almond milk—these are the eighth and ninth ingredients in your love potion.

Invite the one you love to tea or drink it yourself and set an empty place for your loved one. Write his or her name on a heart-shaped piece of red paper and your loved one will soon join you.

Serve hot!

Love-Drawing Sachet

Cut two small pieces of red fabric into identical heart shapes, about 4 inches across. Sew the two pieces together on all sides but leave a small opening. This is called a conjure bag, which is used in many spells. Stuff rosemary into the hole and sew shut. Tuck the sachet inside your bra near your heart to draw love to you.

LOVE DOLL SPELL

by: Dame Darcy

Make a boy doll and a girl doll using the items in this spell. Write all the qualities you want in your perfect person on a piece of red paper and fold it so it fits between the two dolls. Place them facing each other with the girl doll sitting on the boy's lap and bind the red ribbon around them twice, tying it in a bow. As you do, intend to see the perfection in the person you will meet. You will recognize him.

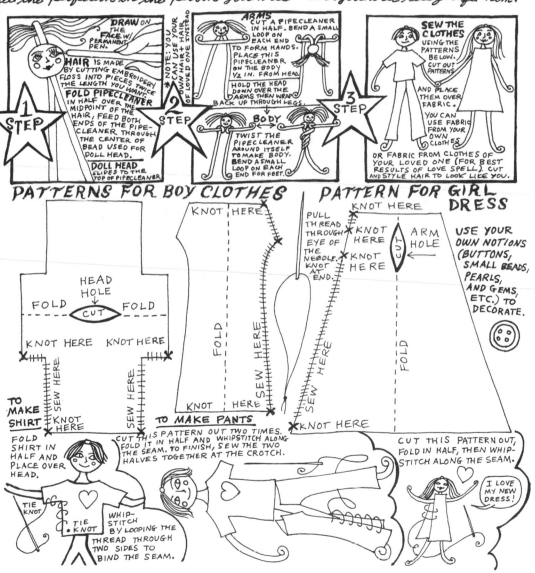

STEP 1

DRAW ON THE FACE W/ PERMANENT PEN.

HAIR IS MADE BY CUTTING EMBROIDERY FLOSS INTO PIECES TWICE THE LENGTH YOU WANT. FOLD PIPECLEANER IN HALF OVER THE MIDPOINT OF THE HAIR, FEED BOTH ENDS OF THE PIPECLEANER THROUGH THE CENTER OF BEAD USED FOR DOLL HEAD.

DOLL HEAD SLIDES TO THE TOP OF PIPECLEANER

* NOTE: YOU CAN USE YOUR OWN HAIR + HAIR OF LOVED ONE INSTEAD

STEP 2

ARMS CUT A PIPECLEANER IN HALF. BEND A SMALL LOOP ON EACH END TO FORM HANDS. PLACE THIS PIPECLEANER ON THE BODY 1/2 IN. FROM HEAD.

HOLD THE HEAD DOWN OVER THE ARMS THEN WRAP BACK UP THROUGH LEGS.

BODY TWIST THE PIPECLEANER AROUND ITSELF TO MAKE BODY. BEND A SMALL LOOP ON EACH END FOR FEET.

STEP 3

SEW THE CLOTHES USING THE PATTERNS BELOW. CUT OUT PATTERNS AND PLACE OVER FABRIC.

YOU CAN USE FABRIC FROM YOUR OWN CLOTHES

OR FABRIC FROM CLOTHES OF YOUR LOVED ONE (FOR BEST RESULTS OF LOVE SPELL). CUT AND STYLE HAIR TO LOOK LIKE YOU.

PATTERNS FOR BOY CLOTHES

HEAD HOLE
FOLD — CUT — FOLD
KNOT HERE   KNOT HERE
SEW HERE
KNOT HERE

TO MAKE SHIRT
FOLD SHIRT IN HALF AND PLACE OVER HEAD.

TIE KNOT   TIE KNOT

WHIPSTITCH BY LOOPING THE THREAD THROUGH TWO SIDES TO BIND THE SEAM.

KNOT HERE
FOLD
SEW HERE
KNOT HERE

TO MAKE PANTS
CUT THIS PATTERN OUT TWO TIMES. FOLD IT IN HALF AND WHIPSTITCH ALONG THE SEAM. TO FINISH, SEW THE TWO HALVES TOGETHER AT THE CROTCH.

PATTERN FOR GIRL DRESS

PULL THREAD THROUGH EYE OF THE NEEDLE. KNOT AT END.

KNOT HERE
KNOT HERE
KNOT HERE
ARM HOLE
CUT
SEW HERE
FOLD
SEW HERE
KNOT HERE

CUT THIS PATTERN OUT, FOLD IN HALF, THEN WHIPSTITCH ALONG THE SEAM.

USE YOUR OWN NOTIONS (BUTTONS, SMALL BEADS, PEARLS, AND GEMS, ETC.) TO DECORATE.

I LOVE MY NEW DRESS!

The Enchantress's Beauty Secrets and Spells

Rag and Pin Curls

Rag and Pin Curls prevent your hair from being tangled at bedtime. Your hair can have a body wave without damage. This practice is centuries old!

1) Cut or rip old bed-sheets into 6-inch-long by 1-inch-wide rags.

40-50 of these will be needed.

FOR PIN CURLS A BOX OF PINS IS NEEDED... ...MAKE SURE THE RUBBER TIPS ARE INTACT.

2) Wash and condition as usual. Comb through with your fingers; let dry to almost complete dryness. Or dampen clean hair with mist.

3) For rag curls, section hair and begin wrapping hair around the rags. Leave extra at the top and end.

↓

Roll the rag curls up and tie into a bow.

4)

5) For pin curls, twist hair into 1-inch sections and secure with bobby pins after rolling hair up to your scalp.

6) Now get a good night's sleep and awake to your dream hair!

NOTICE THE SOFTNESS! →

7) Loose wraps produce a body-wave.

8) Tighter wraps produce curls.

Tips

★ Humidity can affect your hair → bring a clip

★ Don't begin the twist too high up on your head or you will have a crease

HAVE A GOOD HAIR DAY!

Acorn Youth and Beauty Spell

String three acorns together on a silk cord to keep your youth and enhance your beauty. If you have a charm of gold or silver acorns, this will work as well. Let the acorns charge under the new moon and wear them close to you.

Goddess Freya's Potion

Freya's favorite flowers are cowslips (sometimes called primroses). These flowers are also beloved among the fairies and are symbols of beauty.

1. Create an herbal infusion by pouring boiling water over cowslip blossoms.

2. When the water cools, strain out the blossoms.

3. Make sure your potion is completely cool and dab it on your skin with a cotton ball.

4. Use the remainder in a bath.

To Make a Pimple Go Away

Dab on lemon juice or witch hazel. It works. So does garlic juice—but, hey, the smell?

To Soothe Irritated or Sunburned Skin

Mix oatmeal with room-temperature water, make it into a paste, and put it on the skin. As it dries, it takes out the burn and leaves you with a smooth complexion.

How to Make Your Own Makeup

DIY Witch-a-riffic Lip Gloss with Tint

Makes about 35 milliliters (1.2 ounces)

1 teaspoon beeswax pellets

2 teaspoons olive oil

2 tablespoons beet juice or raspberry juice (see note)

Little jars with screw-on tops, such as small jelly jars

½ teaspoon flavoring extract used for baking, like vanilla, peppermint, or almond (optional)

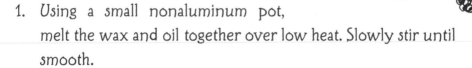

1. Using a small nonaluminum pot, melt the wax and oil together over low heat. Slowly stir until smooth.

2. Remove the pot from the heat, add the juice and, if desired, extract while stirring, and pour the mixture immediately into the containers. Allow it to cool completely before capping and using it. Your new concoction has a shelf life of approximately 6 months and will keep best in a cool place.

Note: To prepare the juice, run beets or raspberries through a juicer. Do not use juice from a store; it has additives that will dilute the tint or inhibit the staining properties you want in your lip gloss.

Glitter Makeup

Mix aloe vera gel with glitter. It's sticky at first and will be easy to apply to your eyelids, arms, cheeks, anywhere! When it dries, the glitter will adhere to your skin so you'll be sparkling all day.

Making SOAP

Glycerin Soap

With glycerin soap you can create exciting soap art and detailed designs. The liquid will pour easily into simple or intricate molds. Try candy molds for some fun shapes. You can also color it any way you want and add dried petals and flowers. After the molding process is complete, you can use your soap right away!

2 cups glycerin soap base
Coloring
Essential oils or fragrance oils
¼ cup cocoa butter
Molds (A bread pan will make a big
    loaf of soap you can slice; candy
    molds will make fun-shaped small soaps.
    You can experiment!)

1. Place the glycerin into a double boiler or slow cooker. Set the heat high enough to make it melt.

2. When the soap base is melted and gooey—don't let it get so hot that it bubbles—you are ready for the color. Add coloring, slowly so the glycerin is evenly tinted and absorbs it all.

3. Now the fun part begins: your signature touch! Stir in your selection of essential oils or fragrance oils slowly, adding only enough to make a pleasant scent, then add the cocoa butter. Make sure to keep stirring until the mixture is very creamy, even, and smooth.

4. When the mixture has blended together completely, carefully pour it into your molds. Wait for the soap to set (it should become hard and dry in a few hours), and then pop it out. You're ready to have good, clean fun—give some soap to your friends too (they will be so impressed)!

For Long, Luxurious Mermaid Hair

A mermaid is a creature who is half woman, half fish. The beauty and elusive mystery of mermaids will always capture mortals' imagination. They are the ultimate symbols of femininity and untamed emotion.

Rinse for Shine

Take a covered pot and boil the following ingredients for five minutes:

$\frac{1}{2}$ cup mint leaves
$\frac{1}{2}$ cup apple cider vinegar
1 cup water

After washing and towel-drying your hair, dip your hairbrush in this rinse and brush through those gorgeous locks.

Deep Conditioning

For a Mexican Fiesta Guacamole Conditioner, mix a spoonful of olive oil with just a dollop of mayonnaise, then add a mashed avocado. Apply to your hair and leave on for 15 minutes. Rinse well with cold water. Decorate your hair with tortilla chips (ha, ha).

How to Have an Enchanted ✦✧✦ Social Life ✦✧✦

To have a true friend, be a true friend. If someone says she likes you one day and hates you the next day, don't take it seriously. Often people who act mean are insecure themselves. Have empathy for them, but avoid them until they treat you with kindness and respect.

Remember that young people are all going through a very intense time of life. Changes are happening to their minds and bodies and making them act crazy and different day to day. When things get hard-core, keep this in mind and try to find a positive outlet for your feelings and energy.

Think of a role model for the kind of person you would like to be, maybe a famous person or someone from history. Read about your role model's life, and when you are in a jam, ask yourself, "What would she do?"

Focus on the things you like to do and try to find something you can be passionate about. Act in a play, go to the skate park, learn how to play an instrument and start a band, take ballet or soccer, join a poetry club or an art or a philosophy class.

When you make friends with all different kinds of people, you won't ever be stereotyped, and you will have a more interesting and well-rounded view of things.

No matter where you are in the popularity ranks, if you believe in yourself, stick up for yourself, and feel and appear confident, you can be unique; people will respect you. Don't take anyone seriously who says or does negative things to you.

Even if you feel insecure, fake it till you make it. Act confident and sassy, and you will win the admiration of everyone around you.

Another way is to create a mystique. Don't let just anyone know who you are.

Start your own parties. Seek out people who seem "familiar" to you. This is the way to recognize your own. Invite them to your magic party, and it won't matter who is having another party with or without you.

Popularity Spell

Do this on a Wednesday, during the waxing moon (when the moon is growing fuller), at three o'clock in the afternoon. (Wednesday is the day ruled by Mercury, so it's good for quickness and communication.)

Place a class photo in a dish—or a photo of anyone you want to be your friend. This spell will charm and enchant a person or a group of people so that they desire to please you. (If you don't have a photo, write the names of the people and anything you know about them.)

Dame Darcy

Mix together licorice leaves, honey, sugar syrup (heated sugar and water), carnation petals, and olive oil.

Pour this mixture over the images or words at the bottom of your dish.

Stir your magic brew while envisioning the perfect scenario with your new friends. Think about what you want, but in a kind and unselfish way, because every loving and good thought has in it the seed of success.

Visualize these scenes, and if you have a fear or negative thought, imagine scissors are cutting around you and your new friends, keeping you together and cutting out the negative person or thought.

While stirring, say these magic words: "Thank you, Divine Spirit, for this perfect day. Miracle shall follow miracle, and wonders shall never end."

Next time you go out, watch for and expect things to change in a positive way. Really believe it, and your world will change in the twinkling of an eye.

Stir your dish once a day for the next three days and then bury the contents under a flowering bush.

Friends Forever Spell

Cut small locks of your hair and the hair of your best friend. Braid them together and tie with pink thread. Place it inside a pink silk conjure bag and keep it in a safe place.

Many Friends Spell

Do this spell on a Wednesday during a waxing moon.

Gather together these items: one long yellow candle (yellow is

the color of social gatherings, fun parties, and happy friendship),
rosemary leaves, dried sage, salt, and sugar. Collect as many sewing pins of various sizes as there are people you want to befriend,
plus one for you.

Mix the rosemary, sage, salt, and sugar in a blender or mortar
and pestle to make friendship powder. Take the powder, the
candle, and the pins outside at noon, during the brightest hour
of the sun. Make a circle of friendship powder, sprinkling it
clockwise around the candle. Push a sewing pin through the
candle and say the name of a person you'd like to befriend as
you do so. Push a second pin through the candle just beneath
the first with the tip pointing up so it forms an X, saying the
name of another friend-to-be.

When you have inserted pins for all the people you want to
befriend, insert one for yourself at the bottom. Then light the
candle. As it burns, the heat, energy, and power from the flame
will first touch the pins representing your friends-
to-be, then yours, bringing you together, for
there is a place where you connect at the center
of the X.

The Enchantress's
✦ ✧ Witch Holidays ✦ ✧

Spring is the season of the Enchantress! Her favorite holidays are all about life, love, and happiness.

Ostara (Spring Equinox)

This celebration of the spring equinox in the Northern Hemisphere occurs on March 20 (March 21 in some years). It is the time when day and night are nearly equal in length. At Ostara, we celebrate the coming of spring and the beginning of new life. Many symbols of fertility and rebirth associated with Ostara (like eggs and bunnies) are a familiar part of Easter celebrations as well. The significance of this time in the year has been noted and celebrated throughout human history.

OSTARA GARDEN

Begin planting your garden on this day. Make sure there are plenty of flowers!

OSTARA EGGS

Write the names of goddesses on hard-boiled eggs with fancy crayon lettering. Fill teacups with warm water, a teaspoon of white vinegar, and a few drops of food coloring. Let your eggs bathe in the tinted water, and the names will appear in relief.

Place the eggs in a basket and have everyone pick one. The name on your egg will indicate your patron goddess for the year to come.

Beltane (May Day)

Beltane is a celebration of life and Mother Earth. As May arrives, the land is in bloom again and passions are stirred! Celebrate by throwing a Beltane party. Choose a May Queen to embody the goddess Flora and make a flower crown for her.

Play a sweet fairy trick and weave together flower wreaths or posies with ribbon to leave on the doorsteps of people you admire. Ring the doorbell and run away as fast as you can so your gifts are a mysterious surprise.

It is said that if you wash your face with dew in the early morning on May 1, you will have a glowing, beautiful complexion all year long.

MAYPOLE DANCE

The Maypole is a fertility symbol (for obvious reasons, hee-hee). Once upon a time, ladies would do a ritual dance, weaving ribbons attached to the Maypole under and over each other. You can re-create this fun dance with your friends.

Dig a post hole in the ground, about two feet deep, then put the Maypole in; any sturdy pole between six and ten feet long will do. Refill the hole with soil so the pole fits snugly and won't fall over. Tie eight to ten multicolored ribbons securely to the top and place a flower wreath there as well (you may want to do this before setting up your pole). For a pole ten feet high, the ribbons should be four yards long. Make sure you have an even number of dancers, then have half the dancers take a ribbon in the right hand and half use the left hand. When the dance begins, each dancer holding a ribbon in the left hand passes under the

ribbon held by the dancer facing her. She then allows the next person coming toward her to pass under her ribbon. She continues this way, alternately passing under a ribbon and then holding her ribbon up so someone can go under it. This way, the ribbon is woven in and out, under and over, all around the pole.

When the ribbons are woven tightly to the pole, the dancers switch hands and unweave them by going the opposite direction.

A MAY DAY SONG

(To be sung in a round as the dancers dance)

Sweet the evening air of May,
Soft my cheek caressing,
Sweet the unseen lilac spray,
With its scented blessing.
White and ghostly in the gloom
Shine the apple trees in bloom.
White and ghostly in the gloom
Shine the apple trees in bloom.

May Day Basket #1
Use this pattern; make it
any size. Cut out on solid
- - - - - - - - - - - - - - - - - - - -
line. Fold on dotted line.
Sew around edge.
Sew ribbons to corners.
Add lace...

Make from Felt or Fabric

#1

#2
Cut this pattern
out × 4, any size;
use felt or card-
board. Sew along
sides and attach
to square bottom.

#2

A Creative Interlude
from the Bard

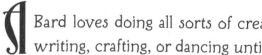 Bard loves doing all sorts of creative things. You'll find her writing, crafting, or dancing until the sun comes up.

✨ Creativity Spell ✨

Brigid is a Celtic saint affiliated with water, fire, and creativity. She particularly helps writers of poetry. She can help unblock your creativity.

Build an altar for her and decorate it with images of cows, pigs, bees, and beehives. Make moon water by setting a jar of water in the light of the full moon to charge it with energy, then place a dish of it at the altar.

Offer Saint Brigid a bowl of milk and black-berries as well as the moon water. When you set this bowl in place, request her assistance with stalled projects or ask her for inspiration.

You can later drink the milk and eat the blackberries.

✳✦† Music: How to Play a Banjo †✳✦

Tuning

The banjo is tuned in an open chord of G. On the guitar, you need to put fingers on the frets to make a chord of G; on the banjo, this is not required. The way I approach tuning is to tune the four long strings like a guitar. You might get help with this from someone who plays the guitar. Musicians seem to find one another.

Right-Hand Rolls (Scruggs Rolls)

When you play a banjo, the thumb picks the top three strings, while the pointer picks the second, and the middle finger picks the bottom. The top string, whose tuning peg is halfway up the banjo's neck, is called the 5 string, and from there to the bottom the strings are 4, 3, 2, and 1. To play a roll, you pick the strings in a particular order. For this one, remember 3251. This means third string (with the thumb), then second string (pointer), fifth string (thumb), and first string (middle finger). Now do it again and again and again: 3251 3251 3251 3251. After a while, the starts and stops will begin to run together, and you will not be able to distinguish between the beginning and ending. It will be one continuous roll: 3251325132513251. This is referred to as the Scruggs roll. With a little practice, you will be able to do it without so much thought.

Now get the roll going slowly and start alternating your thumb on the third and fourth strings, with all other strings in the same order as before. In other words, you will hit the fourth string instead of the third string every other time around: 3251425132514251. This exercise will help you learn to hold a continuous roll while picking out notes to a song.

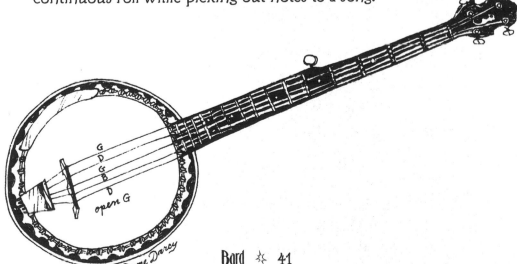

G
D
G
B
D
open G

Dame Darcy

✦✦ Dance: How to Do a Belly Roll ✦✦

Beginning Exercises

Stand with your feet directly below your shoulders, your knees relaxed, and your heart held high. Imagine a string attached to your breastbone, elevating it from the rest of your body.

Place your hands comfortably on your hips.

Now suck in your gut as far as it can go. Then pull it in a little farther. Hold it there as long as you comfortably can.

Now the opposite: relax your belly so much that it protrudes as far forward as it possibly can. Do not push your stomach out. Just relax it and let it all droop forward.

Repeat this exercise several times. Be sure to breathe normally.

Do sit-ups or crunches to build strength in your muscles. The diaphragm controls most of the abdominal work in belly dancing. It should be included in your exercise program. Every breath you take is controlled by your diaphragm.

Try the Roll

Using the above exercises, you learn where your abdominal muscles are and how to control them. The next step is to turn the movement into a roll. Do the first exercise in a graceful, flowing, cyclical movement, with an undulating spirit. Playing slow, sinuous music will help immensely. You may find that circling one direction is easier for you than circling the other. Either is good; ideally you will learn to do both.

Dame Darcy's Feminist Fairy Tales

For centuries, bards passed down folktales from generation to generation. They were masters at memorizing stories word for word, but they also changed bits to fit their own times and audiences. Some of the stories bards told long ago still exist today as modern fairy tales, and these too are continually being changed and updated.

Scattered through this book are some of my own retellings of popular fairy tales, with hot witch twists. Many of the old fairy tales that were written down depict the starring girl waiting for a prince to save her. These feminist fairy tales show the same heroines we all know and love, but this time, they save themselves.

After you read my retellings, have some fun and go write your own!

IF YOU MARRY A HUMAN, YOUR FIN WILL SPLIT INTO TWO LEGS, WHICH IS VERY, VERY PAINFUL. AND EVERY STEP YOU TAKE WILL BE LIKE WALKING ON BROKEN GLASS.

THEN YOU WILL LOSE YOUR VOICE AND NOT BE ABLE TO SPEAK OR SING.

AND FINALLY, IF YOU WANT TO RETURN TO ATLANTIS, OR EVEN SWIM IN THE SEA, YOU WILL BECOME SEA FOAM.

I KNOW THAT FIRST LOVE IS A STRONG THING, AND THEY SAY THE DEEPEST CUT IS THE FIRST CUT. I WOULD RATHER YOU HAVE A TEMPORARY BROKEN HEART THAN LOSE MY PRECIOUS DAUGHTER ALTOGETHER.

THE LITTLE MERMAID THOUGHT OF WHAT HER FATHER SAID AND DECIDED THAT HAVING A VOICE AND BEING ABLE TO SPEAK HER MIND WAS VERY IMPORTANT.

Pagan Priestess

A Pagan is someone in touch with nature, literally "rustic," or "of the country." Pagans believe that everything is interconnected, alive, and divine. Everything has its own spirit. "I salute the divinity in you" is a common Pagan greeting. Pagan Priestesses are champions of diversity, minimal ecological impact, liberty, positive action, responsibility, and equality.

Invitation to the Magic Mother ✦✧† Goddess Dance †✧✦

When I was six, I began going to Catholic school. At the church, kitty-corner from the school, I saw statues of Mother Mary and thought the rainbow patchwork light shining from the stained-glass windows made her so beautiful. At the base of her statue, I could make out words, faintly inscribed, under the serpents and roses where she stood: "Invitation to the Dance of Our Mother Goddess."

I had just learned to read and could also barely see the words, but they rang like a clear bell in my heart. "What do these words mean?" I thought. "Where is the dance? I want to go! The nuns taught me her prayer; maybe the directions were there?" I held my rosary in my slightly sticky, childish grip and contemplated some more. She sort of resembled my own mother, with her long light brown hair parted neatly in the middle and an understanding, empathic gaze. My own mother was a nurse, which meant it was her job, like Mary's, to care about and for people. I thought that there were statues of Mary and none of God because she was the higher authority and the mother of God, thus kind of his "boss," the way my mom was the boss of me.

At the age of six, I instinctively knew the real truth, even though I had no facts yet to back it up. Indeed, the Christian God as we know him has a mother. And for thousands of years, people from all over the world knew and worshipped a mother goddess. Her many names reflect her many roles and ethnicities. Shrines to the Mother date back to the Neolithic Period.

She is the source of all creation as well as destruction. In India her name is Kali; in ancient Greece, Demeter. The Anglo-Saxons called her Ostara; the Norse, Freya. The Egyptians addressed her as Isis.

She is Virgin, Judge, Mother, Bride, and Witch, all melted into one. She is the Queen of the Moon and, like all women, has a right to change her mind. Indeed, she has even more phases than the moon, but that's okay because everything is like that—the trees, seasons, and female bodies, too.

Those who are afraid of all this change think it is chaos, but the Mother just thinks it's fun. She laughs as she stirs her big, swirling soup: the broth made from ocean water and seasoned with salt; stags with long antlers churning past; hawks, butterflies, snails, giant canyons, turning season by season, doing pirouettes in her all-inclusive cauldron. When frightening thunder and lightning perform center stage, the rainbow has a chance afterward to take a beautiful, glittering (rain)bow!

Because her ship was so big and beautiful, and the mermaid masthead so intuitive, ethereal, and not "rational," some macho priests and warriors decided to form a mutiny against Captain Goddess. For many years, and in many cultures, these types of people denied feminine power because it was untidy and unclassifiable.

But fear not, my dears. The happy ending to this ancient tale is that the Goddess is still there and is at this very moment coming back in all her glory. The Goddess, in her typical playful and ironic way, is now dancing with her veils like Salome, throwing them off one by one to reveal a face that we love even more for the fact that her chaotic beauty frightens some men who claim to be modern, even though they are actually obsolete, old, and out of style.

Never mind those fuddy-duddies. They got lost and took the freeway they built, and of course it didn't lead them to the witch party, even though everyone is invited to the Magic Mother Goddess Dance.

And meanwhile we've got a big fire overlooking the ocean here, with glittering stars overhead, garlands of multicolored flowers, and a cornucopia of delicious food. We were born knowing all the steps to the Magic Mother Goddess Dance, and the witches are really letting down their hair now because, after all that work and that long wait, girls just want to have fun!

✦✶† Priestess of the Flowers †✶✦

Botany as Art

Dame Darcy

Preserving Flowers

Temporarily Preserving Cut Flowers

Use an opaque metal, plastic, or glass rectangular container with an airtight lid. The flowers should be dry. Store them in the refrigerator, and they will remain fresh for days.

Drying with Sand

Use colored flowers for this; white flowers will turn yellow as they age. Clean white sand is best. To wash the sand, place about a cup of it at a time in cheesecloth and rinse it until the water running through it is clear. Place the sand on a flat surface such as a cookie sheet and set it in the sun to dry, or dry it in an oven turned on low.

When the sand is fully dry, cut the flowers so the stems are the same length and hold them upright in a leak-free box. Pour enough sand to fill the box to the top of the flower stems. Once the flowers are embedded in the sand up to their petals, make sure that each petal and leaf is in the position you want it to maintain when dried. Carefully pour the rest of the sand over the flowers, filling the box approximately two inches above where the flower tops are.

Set the box in a warm, dry place for two weeks, and do not disturb it. When opening the box, carefully pour the sand out a bit at a time to reveal the dried flowers.

Drying by Hanging

Hang fresh flowers upside down by the end of their stems with a ribbon or thread. This works great with roses!

Pressed Flowers

Place the flower in the position you want it to dry, between two blank sheets of paper inside a really thick book. Don't forget to remove the flower later, even though it is so sweet, sad, and romantic to find a pressed flower from a lovelorn girl of long ago between the pages of an antique book.

To begin your own herbarium scrapbook, take the flower after it has dried and paint the back with school glue or paste. Press it carefully on a page in a blank book or on a sheet of paper that you can combine with other pages to make a book. You can also make greeting cards, valentines, or place cards for a tea party using this method.

Decorating with Flowers

Glitter Flowers

Water down school glue to a paintlike consistency and paint dried flowers with it. Sprinkle glitter on the wet glue. Or paint your flowers with glitter nail polish.

Rosewater

For each handful of rose petals, you will need one quart of water. Simmer the water and petals on low, stirring occasionally until the essence of rose has infused the water. Pour into bottles and let your tincture sit for three days. You can either filter the water through cheesecloth or let the petals remain in the water. Use the rosewater in the bath or put it in a spray bottle to scent your clothing or spritz your face during hot weather.

Sachets

Sew two squares of fine, semitransparent fabric on three sides using a running stitch. Fill the open side with dried flowers and sew closed. These can be put in your dresser drawer or anywhere to impart a fresh scent.

Ink and Paint Leaf Prints

Find a leaf that appeals to you. Making sure it is free of dust and moisture, spread tempera paint evenly across the leaf and place it on a sheet of paper. Lay another piece of paper over the back of the leaf and set a heavy book on top. After a few moments, carefully remove the book, paper, and leaf to reveal the print.

Put several pages of leaf prints together to form a book, or cut the leaves from the paper and hang them from strings tied to crossed and bound sticks to make a mobile.

Print multiple leaves arranged in a row to make a natural-looking branch, and fill the spaces between the leaves by painting a simple line. With small leaves, this can be used to ornament handmade stationery and envelopes or the corners of a scrapbook.

Flower Patterns

Magic symbols are found in flowering plants. A spiral is seen in a galaxy, and also in the spiral of the rose. The lotus is an important symbol of transformation because its stem is rooted in and feeds off the dark muck beneath the water. Through its stem, the lotus transforms the muck into a beautiful flower blossoming in the light. When you cut an apple in half horizontally, you find a star (or pentagram), which is a symbol of creation and life because it looks like a human being, with a head, two arms, and two legs.

Use the spiral, the layers of the lotus leaves, and the pentagram to design patterns. When you exaggerate these patterns, you can come up with some amazing, original designs. Embroider the designs on clothing, paint them on china cups, print them to make wallpaper—whatever you're inspired to create.

✨✦ A Pagan Priestess Garden ✦✨

Before You Start

WHAT TO GROW

Think about what you want to grow. Take into consideration your climate, local pests, soil, and what you like to cook. Classic food plants are kale, green beans, and carrots. Tomatoes are versatile and can make great salsa or marinara sauce for pasta. Spice up your life by growing parsley, basil, rosemary, and sunflowers. Luffa gourds can be grown and used as sponges.

BASIC EQUIPMENT

Depending on what you are growing and where, you may need a shovel, hoe, rake, wire and wire cutters, stakes, fencing, wheelbarrow, hose, watering can, baskets to put produce in, and peat pots. A cool, dark storage area is great for keeping produce. You may also want canning jars, boiling pots, and equipment for drying and grinding, and if you have an apple tree, a hand press for apple cider. Don't forget the gardening books!

Preparing the Soil

COMPOSTING

Good compost improves the quality of the soil in your garden. Make compost from old leaves, vegetable leftovers, and coffee grounds. Seaweed or other sea vegetation is great for compost. Do not use meat scraps or bones; they attract animals and smell awful as they break down.

Put the compost materials into a trough dug into the ground and lined with plastic, a bathtub sunk in the ground, or a perforated trash can with lid. Make sure your compost is covered at all times; this will encourage decomposition and prevent flies from breeding.

Your compost will be ready to use after six months or sooner if you turn it periodically.

When adding compost to soil, break up the earth clods with a hoe. Throw in the compost and turn it under.

MULCHING

Mulch, which can be made from layers of sawdust, straw, leaf mold, or wood chips, will protect the soil from drying out and conserves water. Apply a layer one inch thick, leaving a half inch clear around the base of the stems.

Planting

PREPARING SEEDLINGS

Seedlings are fragile and can freeze if they are out in cold weather. To prevent this, grow them indoors first, and then plant them in the early spring after the last frost.

Take an egg carton and use half of an eggshell in each cup. Poke a little hole in the bottom of each eggshell with a pin for drainage. Fill the eggshell with organic potting soil and make a small hole in the soil with your pinkie. Plant a few seeds in each hole and cover again with the soil.

Place the egg carton in a window and water the cups every other day. When your outdoor garden is prepared and the eggshells contain small leaf shoots, they are ready to be planted.

Create a little ecosystem and protection for your young plants by putting a glass jar over them until they're large enough to fend for themselves.

STAGGER YOUR PLANTING

Read the seed packets for specific directions. You will have a continuous supply of food when you plant each crop over a series of weeks.

Harvest

When your foods have ripened, pick and enjoy!

Dame Darcy

Raw Food Recipes

You can use some of the foods from your garden in these raw food recipes. When you eat raw food, you use unprocessed fresh ingredients and none of the nutrients are lost to the heat of cooking. It's like those mud pies you made as a kid, but you can really eat it this time! Raw food is ecofriendly fairy food.

You can use a regular blender for these recipes, but be sure to chop everything as much as possible and feed the blender gradually so you won't break it. When making something particularly gooey, you'll need to stop the blender now and again and stir it before giving it another go.

HUMMUS

Blend in a blender...

1 can chickpeas
1/4 cup virgin olive oil
salt (a pinch)

1-2 tablespoons lime
or lemon juice

hot pepper
2-5 cloves garlic
dry parsley leaves

eat with baby carrots,
celery, cherry tomatoes

Love
Dame Darcy

DRESSING

1 CUP OLIVE OIL
1 TEASPOON HONEY
1/4 CUP LEMON JUICE
1/3 CUP WATER
1 CUP CHOPPED HERBS
(PARSLEY, CILANTRO, BASIL)

1/3 CUP SEEDS OR NUTS OR TAHINI
SEA SALT
SPICE → GARLIC, GINGER,
MUSTARD

BLEND IN BLENDER

Love
Dame Darcy

RAW ICE CREAM SUNDAE

★ Cut three bananas into circle slices ～ put them in a covered container ～ freeze them.

★ Feed them a bit at a time through the hole in the blender lid as you blend.

★ Also add coconut cream gradually ～ add ½ a can. ～

★ Cut a banana in half ～ place each half in a sundae dish. ～

★ Scoop the ice cream into the dish. ～ (For flavors: when ice cream is still in blender, add baking chocolate / cocoa powder or vanilla extract, fresh strawberries, etc.)

★ Add fresh fruit, berries, nuts, bee pollen sprinkles, and a cherry on top!

★ To make Chocolate Sauce: Blend real maple syrup with cocoa powder

★ Whipped cream is the rest of the can of coconut cream, blended.

Dame Darcy

Do–It–Yourself
✦✧✦ Pagan Priestess Tips ✦✧✦
Simple Sewing

RUNNING STITCH

This stitch will sew anything together simply and quickly. Thread a needle, line up both ends of the thread evenly, and then fasten the ends in a double-tied knot. Line up the pieces of fabric you wish to sew together and push the needle through both, pulling until the knot is against the fabric. Push the needle back through the fabric to make the first stitch. Repeat, making all your stitches the same length. When you've finished sewing, loop the needle through the thread to make a knot against the fabric. Double tie it for strength and cut off the ends of the thread.

1. Thread needle and make both sides even

2. Knot at the end

3. Push needle through alternating sides of fabric to make running stitch

WHIPSTITCH

Attach the edges of two pieces of fabric together by always pushing the needle through the same side of the fabric. Insert the needle and pull until the knot is against the fabric, then loop the thread around both pieces; move down a space and repeat the stitch. Continue this way for as long as necessary to make your seam. If you want the seam to be invisible, sew on the side you don't want to see and turn the fabric inside out.

How to Make a Rag Rug

Here's a fun project that uses the whipstitch.

Take long strips of fabric about two inches wide and tie them together. Continue until you have three very long ropes of tied fabrics.

Tie one end of the ropes to something or have someone hold them. Plait the strips into a thick braid. Coil the braid, and whipstitch the coil securely to itself on both sides of the braid.

You can make rugs for large areas or mini bath mats this way, depending on how many fabric strips you use.

Knitting

Knitting has multiple witchcraft connections. You are making a series of knots, and knots retain power, as do braids. You are also taking one continuous length of yarn and crafting and transforming it into something else. The warmth of knitwear comes from the heart.

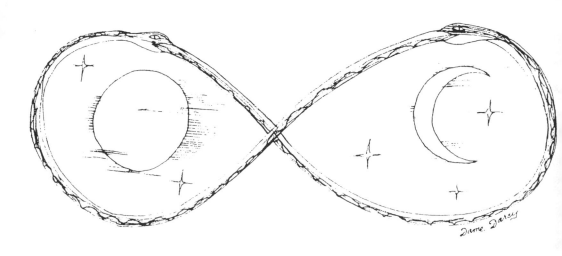

Casting On

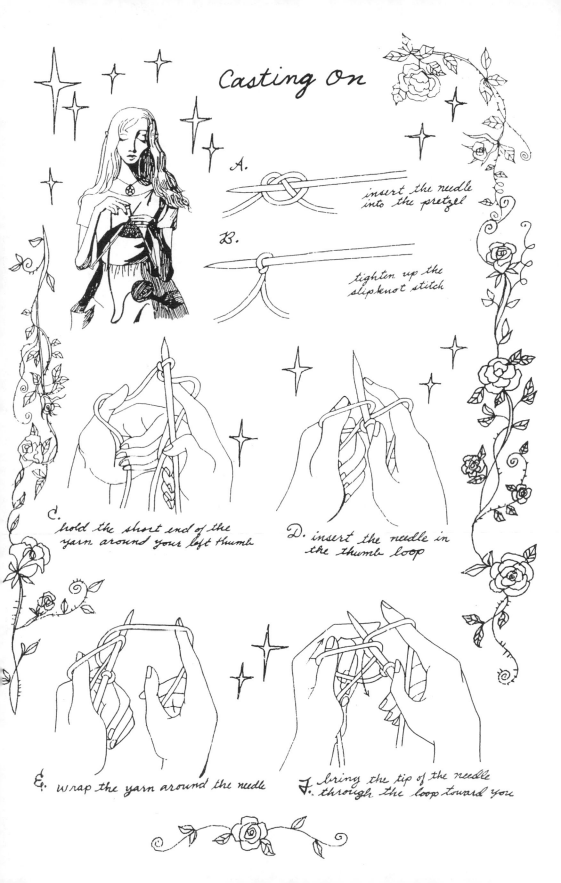

A. insert the needle into the pretzel

B. tighten up the slipknot stitch

C. hold the short end of the yarn around your left thumb

D. insert the needle in the thumb loop

E. wrap the yarn around the needle

F. bring the tip of the needle through the loop toward you

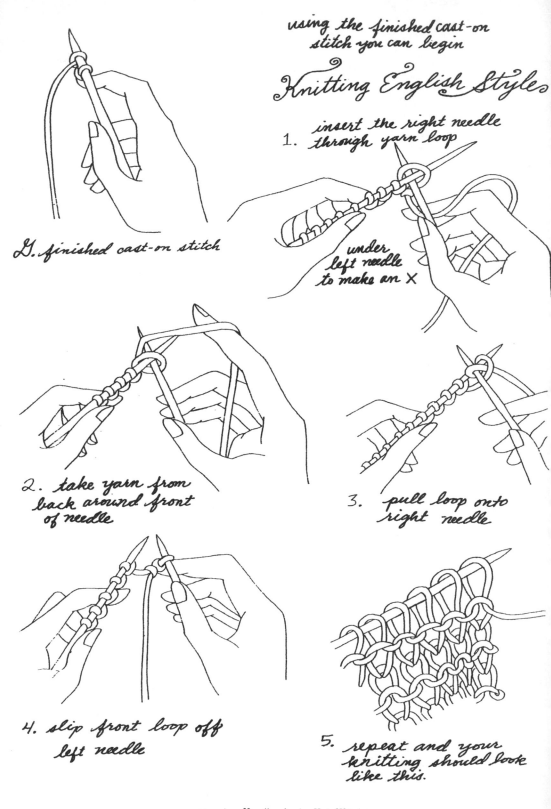

using the finished cast-on stitch you can begin

Knitting English Styles

1. insert the right needle through yarn loop

D. finished cast-on stitch

under left needle to make an X

2. take yarn from back around front of needle

3. pull loop onto right needle

4. slip front loop off left needle

5. repeat and your knitting should look like this.

Basic Knit Cast Off

1

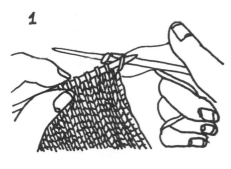

Knit the first two stitches from the left needle onto the right. Keep the yarn to the back of your knitting. Insert the left needle through the base of the first stitch on the right needle from left to right.

2

Pick up the stitch, bring it over the top of the second stitch, and slip it off the right needle.

3

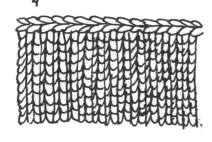

With one stitch left over on your right needle, knit the next stitch from your left needle and repeat until one stitch remains. Afterward, cut the yarn, leaving a 6-inch (15cm) tail. Draw this remaining yarn through the last stitch and pull it tight.

4

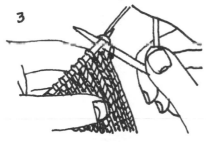

good luck

have fun!

Love Dame Darcy

Candle Making

Warning! Do not burn candles near or directly on anything wooden or fabric. Burn candles away from drafts and never leave them unattended.

Beeswax Candles

Taking a long, flat sheet of beeswax, place the wick on one side of the sheet and roll the wax tightly around the wick. Beeswax gives off a pleasant honey smell when lit.

Scented Candles

Melt wax in a double boiler, then pour a few drops of essential oil into it and mix well. Good scents to use are clove, rose, cinnamon, vanilla, or lavender. Anchor a wick to the bottom of an empty small milk carton by tying it to a heavy magnet or something similar. Then tie the other end of the wick around a pencil and balance it across the top of the carton. Pour the wax mixture into the carton. When the wax dries, cut the carton away, and you will be left with a square candle.

Simple Stained-Glass Lantern

Choose a glass jar large enough to hold your scented candle without the flames touching the glass. Using wax crayons, color a piece of paper in a stained-glass design. Wrap the paper around the outside of the jar and tape it into place. Place the candle in the jar, light it, and enjoy the glowing colors.

DRUID
Spotlight on ✦✧✦ a Pagan ✦✧✦

Druids

Druids were highly spiritual, skilled, and intellectual, and were the elite of pagan Celtic society. Druids were in touch with nature and nature spirits, such as fairies.

Summoning Fairies

DRUID FAIRY HILL SUMMONING

For centuries, fairy kingdoms have been known to reside in mounds, hills, and mountains that are hollow.

Once you have identified the hill, walk around it counterclockwise three times, saying, "Open door!"

LUCKY CLOVER FAIRY SUMMONING

After finding a four-leaf clover, lay seven grains of wheat on it while focusing on your desire. The fairies will appear and grant your wish.

The Pagan Priestess's
✦ Witch Holidays ✦

Summer is a great time to be out of doors in nature—so it is a great time to be a Pagan Priestess!

Litha (Midsummer's Eve)

June 21 (or sometimes June 20), the summer solstice, is the longest day of the year. It is a celebration of the sun and the beginning of summer.

As in the Shakespeare play *A Midsummer Night's Dream*, fairies, elves, brownies, leprechauns, and all other creatures from the land of the Fae are said to come awake this evening. Leave a little cup of milk and honey out for them in a fairy circle of flowers and trees, near a hole in a tree, balanced on a mushroom table, by a little brook, or anywhere you feel they dwell. When you return, if the milk and honey are gone, they have accepted your offering. You will have the luck of the fairies with you, and magic things will abound in your life!

Have a midsummer's eve party and make a cake using the fruit of the season. Mead (honey wine) is traditionally sipped on this night, but iced strawberry, chamomile, or hibiscus tea with honey can be substituted easily. Play midsummer games!

THE INVISIBLE FERN GAME

Before this game, explain the legend of the fern seeds: on the night of Litha, the invisible seeds of a fern can be gathered, and when you have them on you, they will render you invisible.

Then blindfold everyone except for one person. This is the person who receives the fern frond.

The other players stand in a circle, holding hands around the magic fern bearer. They circle to the right three times, saying, "Around goes the year, midsummer is here," and then to the left three times, saying, "Bad luck will turn to good luck with the fern." Then they walk forward into the circle and let go of their hands.

Dame Darcy

The players reach toward the person in the center and the fern. They all pull their blindfolds off to reveal who is now holding or is closest to the fern. This is the person who wins summer solstice good luck and is to be rewarded with a green ribbon or good luck card.

THE WHEEL OF FORTUNE

Use a hula hoop as the wheel and choose someone to say the spell while attendees stand in a big circle about two feet from one another. The hoop is passed by rolling it from one person to the next in the circle. Each person passes the wheel on a line of the spell.

> *Midsummer, hear this mystic song.*
> *Please guide the wheel of fortune along.*
> *Bring power, happiness, fame, and wealth,*
> *Long life, good friends, true love, and health,*
> *Abundance and successful music and art,*
> *With a full and happy heart.*

If the wheel does not go directly to the next player, if it stops, or if the player fails to catch it or touch it as it passes, that person must leave the circle. The last word said in the poem before the hoop went wrong hints at the main problem that player will have this year. The player left standing at the end is the winner, and the good luck of the mythical midsummer fairies will be bestowed on that Fortune's Favorite.

Lúnasa (Summer Equinox)

Also Known as Lammas ("Loaf Mass")

This August 1 holiday is named for the Celtic god of the sun. It is a sun-worshipping witch holiday, but it also marks the start of the turn toward autumn, so it is sort of a melancholy holiday as well.

Lúnasa is the first of three witch harvest holidays, and we celebrate by baking loaves of bread from the season's first harvest. The sun rays caught in the wheat are then eaten, the bread representing the fallen body of the sun god.

MAGIC DOLLS

by: Dame Darcy

QUILTED Pillow Doll

USING THIS PATTERN, CUT OUT FRONT AND BACK OF DOLL IN SOFT MATERIAL. SEW TOGETHER AROUND EDGE OF DOLL. TURN INSIDE OUT TO HIDE SEAM. FILL WITH COTTON FOR PADDING. X MARKS WHERE THREAD STARTS AND STOPS. STITCH DOLL FRONT AND BACK TOGETHER ON DOTTED LINES.

EMBROIDER HAIR, EYES, AND MOUTH.

SATIN STITCH

CHAIN STITCH

SOFT AND COZY!

MAGIC BOTTLE DOLL

1. WRITE WISH. MAKE A PIECE OF PAPER INTO A FUNNEL. POUR SAND INTO THE BOTTOM OF THE BOTTLE AND FILL THE REST WITH SCRAP FABRIC.

2. FORM THE DOLL'S HEAD OVER THE BOTTLE NECK USING AIR-DRY CLAY. WRAP WIRE AROUND TOP OF BOTTLE.

3. TIE STRIPS OF FABRIC TO THE ENDS OF THE WIRE AND WRAP TIGHTLY TO MAKE ARMS.

4. SECURE YARN WITH CRAFT GLUE FOR HAIR. PAINT FACE.

5. MAKE "A-LINE" DRESS— SEW AND TURN INSIDE OUT TO HIDE SEAMS. ALTER SIZE OF PATTERN TO FIT BOTTLE, IF NEEDED. SEW TRIM OR OTHER DETAILS. TIE BOW AT BACK TO CINCH WAIST.

MAGIC

fairyPrincess Doll

SUPPLIES: YARN, WOODEN BEAD, PAINT OR PENS FOR FACE, GLUE.

STEP 1
CUT SEVERAL LENGTHS OF YARN. FOLD IN HALF AND TIE WITH A BOW, CREATING A LOOP.

STEP 2
SEPARATE THE LOOP INTO THREE SECTIONS.

STEP 3
PUSH CENTER SECTION OF LOOP THROUGH HOLE IN BEAD. CUT LOOP TO CREATE HAIR. GLUE, THEN STYLE.

STEP 4
TIE YARN AROUND OTHER TWO LOOPS TO CREATE WINGS. PAINT OR DRAW FACE WITH PEN.

hot witch sleeping beauty

by: Dame Darcy

"THIS IS DEPRESSING," SLEEPING BEAUTY SAID TO HERSELF AS SHE LAY IN A COMA-LIKE STATE, HOLDING HER DOLL.

"DESPITE THESE COBWEBS SHROUDING MY FACE LIKE AN INTRICATE GORGEOUS VEIL."

SHE LOOKED LIKE THE MOST GLORIOUS QUEEN OF THE GOTHS LIKE THAT, WITH HER BLACK HAIR FLOWING AROUND HER AND DOWN THE BED.

THE LIGHT BARELY FILTERED THROUGH THE STAINED-GLASS WINDOWS OF THE CASTLE, AND THE HUGE BRIARS THAT THE WITCH'S CURSE HAD GROWN MADE IT NO BETTER. THEY COMPLETELY BLOCKED OUT THE SUN, NOT THAT SLEEPING BEAUTY COULD SEE THROUGH HER EYELIDS ANYWAY.

SHE HAD BEEN WAITING A CENTURY FOR THAT STUPID PRINCE CHARMING.

"BY THE TIME HE WAKES ME UP, I'LL BE 100 YEARS OLDER THAN HIM, AND WE ALL KNOW HOW GIRLS MATURE FASTER THAN BOYS. DOES THAT MAKE ME A COUGAR?"

HER LITHE LIMBS, ONCE VERY ADEPT AT SPINNING, KNITTING, AND OTHER CRAFTS, WERE BECOMING ATROPHIED (THOUGH PALE IN A LOVELY, SURREAL WAY). SHE TRIED TO LIFT THEM... AND COULDN'T.

"DRAT!" SHE THOUGHT.

SHE DREAMED OF HER LIFE BEFORE THE WITCH PUT A CURSE ON HER FAMILY....

"IF ONLY MOTHER HAD NOT BEEN SO RUDE TO THAT EVIL WITCH... ALL SHE WANTED WAS EQUAL TREATMENT. WHY DID THEY HAVE TO GO AND SHUN HER LIKE THAT, JUST BECAUSE HER SKIN GLOWED IN THE DARK!"

Mystic

Mystics are highly spiritual, profound people in touch with the magical world to the highest degree. Using her vast experience, a Mystic can *see* through anything to its core of truth, and she has very strong intuitive powers beyond rational explanation.

✨✝ Places of Magic ✝✨

The ordinary world is not all there is to be seen. Fairies and spirits exist in a magical world alongside our reality. It is the acknowledgment of and communication with these beings and this world of spirits that separates people living in one level of normal reality from a witch who has mastered magic. Mystics are especially adept at walking the path between the worlds.

There are certain places that are particularly good for casting spells and contacting spirits because they are close to the realm of magic.

Fairy Ring

A ring of flowers or trees. Anyone who steps inside is transported to the realm of the Fae. The person who experiences this may find herself skipping through time, able to see and hear fairies.

Rainbow

The refraction of white light into separate colors is a symbol of transformation. The symbolic gold at the end of the rainbow represents enlightenment.

Haunted House

Stairs in a haunted house are a place where the veil of reality is particularly thin, so one can talk to ghosts (spirit people who

have "crossed over"). Stairs work as a portal because they are on neither one floor nor the other.

Forest

Trees are alive, and they have their own history and life force. Ancient woods were sacred to early pagans, as they are to us today, and are a wonderful place to reconnect with life's spirit.

Ocean

A whole other world—there are endless sunken mountains and alien life forms in the deepest uncharted depths of the ocean, which is as mysterious and unknown to us as outer space.

Magic Circles

Create a magic circle to perform rituals. This makes a door into the other world that will close after the ritual is performed, or a circle of safety or invisibility around you or your property when needed.

Dream World

Dreams, lucid dreaming, meditation, and self-hypnosis can help you identify and alter your mind and emotions, then rid you of negativity so you can manifest a positive reality.

✦✧✦ Creating Your Own Magical Space ✦✧✦

Building an Altar

Find a place where your altar will not be disturbed. It can even be a small shelf mounted on the wall.

On a balanced altar, the four elements will be represented—fire, air, earth, and water—as well as spirit. You can change your altar depending on what you want to use it for. Altars can help focus magical energy in spells and rituals. Ask the aid of elements or deities you admire. Put down an altar cloth to suit your magical color needs.

For the water element, include water, tea, or something else to drink in a cup or a chalice. Or you can use a small fishbowl, shells, or coral.

For the earth element, an offering of food is great, as long as it's fresh. Or put fresh flowers or a plant in a pot or a vase. Special rocks, crystals, or stones also represent the earth element.

For the air element, feathers, a bell, or a butterfly is a good start.

To represent the fire element on your altar, use a statue of a dragon, a red or orange gem, a lava rock, or charred wood. Or an unlit red candle.

To represent spirit, find and hang pictures and statues of deities. My favorites are Mami Wata, the Black Madonna, and Hecate. I also like the gods of love Cupid and Aphrodite.

Now hang photos of people and things you like, magic totem animals, or a crystal to refract light and add a rainbow to your altar. This is also the place to put your moon water, herbs, and anything else that you want to keep in a safe place and charge with energy.

Create or find your own mantra. This is a sentence or a word you can say once or repeatedly until you feel a shift in your consciousness and heart. Say it while you do your rituals or just as you sit at and attend to your altar. It will help you feel better and stronger and let go of worries and stress.

For some examples of mantras, see the Mystical Meditations section.

Casting a Ritual Circle

Ritual circles are places of power, where magic comes more easily and the veil between the worlds is thinner. Circle casting grants the tools on the altar the powers of earth, air, fire, water, and spirit. Together these create the circle of life and our sacred space. Cast spells within magic circles, or meditate, or make up your own rituals with your friends.

To spiritually prepare for any ritual, first fill a chalice with salt water. Then walk around the area you wish to contain in a clockwise direction, sprinkling the water to cast the circle. Have any attendants at the ritual hold hands in the center as you cast the circle. Call out to the spirits as you reach the corresponding points of the compass.

We call to the Spirits of the East and Air:
  we bid you welcome; enter our circle.
We call to the Spirits of the South and Fire:
  we bid you welcome; enter our circle.
We call to the Spirits of the West and Water:
  we bid you welcome; enter our circle.
We call to the Spirits of the North and Earth:
  we bid you welcome; enter our circle.
We call to the Spirits Above, to the high beings of the cosmos
  and other worlds: we bid you welcome; enter our circle.
We call to the Spirits Below, to the ancestors and the ancient
  ones: we bid you welcome; enter our circle.
We call to the Spirits of the Center, to the spark of light that
  meets and merges within each of us: we bid you wel-
  come; enter our circle.
We would also like to welcome to our circle loved ones who
  have passed on, spirit helpers, guides, and higher selves.
The circle is cast and is a safe space. We are now between
  worlds; what happens between worlds affects all worlds.

When the ritual is complete, undo the circle by saying the
following:

We thank you, Spirits of the East, South, West, North, Above,
  Below, and Center. The circle is open but unbroken.

✦✦✦ Cats as Mystics ✦✦✦

Cats are astute, adept, clever, secretive, mysterious, intelligent, intuitive, supernatural, watchful, selective, independent, and don't forget cute and cuddly! They were beloved by the ancient Egyptians, who even mummified their favorite felines so they would last far into the future. Cats symbolize feminine traits, and how someone treats cats is a reflection on how they treat girls. In medieval times, many innocent cats were burned along with innocent girls who were accused of witchcraft because they showed independent, catlike traits. A black cat is not bad luck as some people say—these cats have the most magical, mystical powers. For starters, they can see in the dark and disappear!

Dame Darcy

✦✧✦ Mystical Meditations ✦✧✦

Recognize Your Desires

If you feel envy or resentment because of what others have, remember that it is a sign you are recognizing what you want. You could be next in line; recognizing what you want is the first step toward getting it. Success is not a secret; it is a system. The road to success lies in being truly interested in what you do and being self-interested in a good, productive way.

The Power of Words

Ali Baba's treasure was hidden behind barriers of rock and stone. To access it, all he needed to do was exclaim out loud his magic words "open sesame!" and his barriers moved aside.

This story shows how powerful the right words can be. Speak and manifest self-affirming phrases out loud every day:

> Every moment brings prosperity and abundance;
>   I now see all the signs.
> Inner peace guides me and draws all my desires to me.

If you are tired of waiting and living in a way that you feel is stifling, say,

> Waiting is over, no more barriers surround me;
>   I step forward into my garden of earthly delights
>   and enjoy the roses of my success.

Release Your Problems

Recognize your mental tension; clearly focus on what it is you want to address. Feel where you hold that in your body, and when you breathe in, visualize the clear, cleansing white light of oxygen coming in through your breath. Bathe your problem in this, and then release it with your exhalation. Visualize it as black smoke and impurities being removed from you.

Spells to Grant Wishes and Desires

MAGNETISM Spells

First, in a quiet space, sit upright in a chair and visualize a rod or beam that is hollow like a tube stretching through your spine up to the heavens. This connects you to the universe above and also goes down into the earth, grounding you.

Close your eyes and breathe through your nose, focusing only on your breathing. If any thought comes into your mind, put it in a pink bubble and pop the bubble with the word *thought*. Do this as many times as needed until you have a clear mindscape.

To clear yourself of baggage, imagine actual baggage going down the tube from you into the ground and disappearing somewhere far away. You can also imagine sand or black smoke or anything else that represents the negative energy you want to clear.

You are now ready to magnetize your objects of power.

Manifestation Ring

Get a ring you like. It doesn't have to be an expensive one; any costume jewelry, rhinestone ring will do. Hold it in your hand and really look at it, memorizing every detail. Now close your eyes and see the ring in your mind's eye.

While you are holding the ring, picture a coil deep inside you. It rotates around the beam grounding you to the earth and sky. Imagine it to be a warm color like red or orange. Feel it turn clockwise in your body and heat up like the coil in a space heater.

With each rotation, the feeling of magnetism becomes stronger; now picture the ring you have in your hand. What is your favorite stone or your birthstone? Visualize the ring in your hand turning into a ring with that stone; imagine how you would feel with that ring on your finger.

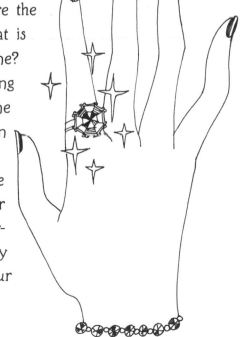

When all feelings of doubt are gone and you feel certain about your manifestation of the ring, say to yourself, "Now is the time. I accept my greatest gift." When you open your eyes, know with certainty that you will receive the ring. Now your only task is to keep on the lookout for it. When it is given to you, put it on your finger and say thank you.

You will now have a magic ring as a daily reminder of your manifestation and magnetism magic. Now when you have a request or a wish that you want to magnetize, do the Magnetism Meditation while holding the request written on a piece of paper in the hand on which you wear the magic ring. Repeat this process as many times as you want until you have everything your heart desires.

Door to Success

Use the same techniques to magnetize a doorknob. You can use any doorknob you like: one of colored cut glass, one of old-fashioned embellished brass, or a perfectly round one that looks like a crystal ball.

When you do your meditation, hold the doorknob in your hand and visualize it becoming empowered with the word *yes*. When you open your eyes, know with certainty that you will receive anything you request.

For instance, if you are going to a party where you want to make new friends, before you open the real door to go in to the party, place your magic doorknob on the door and turn it, saying, "Nothing is too good to be true. I am open to receiving everything my heart desires." Then, slipping the doorknob into your purse safely out of sight, walk into the room and greet your new friends.

This applies to anything you once had uncertainty about. It will give you the power to magnetize, manifest, and own any new reality in life you want. Put the magic doorknob on the door to any job you want, turn it, and when you walk into the office, you will have the position you desire. Place the magic doorknob on the dean's office of any school you want, and you will get in. Put the magic doorknob on the door to the home of your new boyfriend or friend, and they will let you in and form a magic bond with you.

Never tell anyone about the Manifestation Ring or show the Door to Success to anyone except perhaps your most trusted witch sister. If you keep your magic to yourself, it remains crystal clear and unclouded by other people's intentions.

How to Make a Sigil

The purpose of a sigil is to manifest a wish into reality.

1. Write your wish on a piece of paper.
2. Look through the words of your wish, crossing out any repeating letters.
3. The letters that are left are the ones you will use to make the sigil.
4. Combine the curves of letters like S and O and the lines of letters like T and X to form your own symbol.

HOW TO MAKE
A SIGIL

HOW TO MAKE
A SIGIL

5. Write the symbol on a piece of paper and fold it four times.
6. Bury it under a blossoming tree, a bush, or even a flowerpot.
7. Your wish is granted!

My Wallet Is Always Full Spell

Always keep a leaf from a bay laurel tree with your money, and your wallet or purse will never be empty.

✴✦✝ The Mystic's Witch Holidays ✝✦✴

Autumn is a time of change, a time when the wall between the magical and real worlds grows thin. Mystics, already in touch with the magical world, are especially powerful in autumn.

Mabon (Autumn Equinox)

This September 22 (or sometimes September 23) holiday is the second of three witch harvest festivals (the first is Lúnasa and the last is Samhain).

As with its opposing sister holiday, the springtime Ostara, day and night are the same length during Mabon. This is a traditional time for having a feast day or thanksgiving.

Samhain (Halloween)

This is the Witches' New Year. Opposite to Beltane (which takes place on May 1), Samhain is considered the other most important Witch holiday because it is when we finish harvesting what we have planted and start anew.

November 1, the day after Samhain, is also known as All Saints' Day. Fairies, ghosts, and all sorts of mysterious and supernatural creatures are known to be around at this time.

The Witching Hour is the midnight between these two days, when Halloween shifts to All Saints' Day. This is a time when the barriers between the world of the real and that of the surreal are thin. Thus, it is the best evening to practice magic and to divine the future that the New Year will bring.

DIVINING SHIP OF LIGHT

Cut a length of candlewick, place it in the center of a nutshell, and pour melted wax around it. When the wax has dried, you will have a little floating candle boat. Prepare one of these for each of the party guests.

Fill a tub full of water and have two guests light their boats and place them in the tub. Stir the water with a stick and watch the boats.

If the light of the candle burns steadily, a joyful and lengthy life is expected.

If two boats meet and sail together, these friends will remain side by side throughout their lives.

When two boats come into each other's space it means the friends will have similar tastes and will meet periodically over the course of their lives to share their affinity.

If one boat crosses the path of another, it means the people will do the same in life.

If a boat stays at the side of the tub, declining to venture into the deep water of the middle, this means the person will stay close to home and not be the adventurous type.

MAGIC MIRROR

How many lucky breaks will you get this year? You can find out on the full moon closest to Halloween. Stand indoors at an open door or window where you can see the moon. Hold a mirror into the light of the moon and gaze into the mirror. Count the number of times the moon is reflected. This dictates the number of lucky breaks you will get in the next year.

LIGHT AS A FEATHER, STIFF AS A BOARD

One girl lies on the floor as straight as she can with her arms to her sides. The other girls surround her, putting only two fingers under her on all sides. They chant slowly and quietly together, "Light as a feather, stiff as a board," and eventually the center girl will float above the floor, rising slowly up with only the power of the other girls' fingers.

BLOODY MARY

If you have a big mirror or a wall mirror, this game is great for the whole party. One girl turns her back to the mirror (while the others watch), holding the candle or flashlight under her chin so the light reflects her face. Everyone chants "Bloody Mary" slowly and with conviction three times. When the girl with the candle turns around to look at her reflection in the mirror, the face of Bloody Mary will be seen instead. What does Bloody Mary look like? You'll see . . . ha ha ha!

BOBBING FOR APPLES

Fill a tub with water and float some apples in it. Try to grab them with your teeth only. The winner gets a prize.

FIND THE GHOSTLY FLAME

Light a candle. In an adjoining room, place a blindfold over the players' eyes and then lead them into the room with the candle. Their objective is to find the candle and blow out the flame. The other party guests can let the blindfolded ones know if they are close by saying "hot" or "cold." When the candle is blown out, the game is won.

BLIND MAN'S BLUFF

A player is blindfolded and stands in the center of a circle, wildly grabbing at the others around her. The one who is caught becomes the next blind man.

Día de los Muertos (Day of the Dead)

In Mexico, the Day of the Dead is celebrated in conjunction with All Saints' Day, on November 1 and 2. It is a time to recognize our temporary existence in this life and to honor our ancestors. Shrines to the dead are made using their photos and small statues of skeletons depicting things they did during life. Painted sugar skulls, marigolds, and altar candles also are contributed to the shrine.

On Día de los Muertos, say a prayer to your ancestors and light a candle in their honor. Write your burden, worry, or concern on a piece of paper and ask the dead to bear it away. Light it with a candle, put it in a cauldron or bowl, and watch it burn completely.

Take the ashes to a graveyard and throw them to the wind or bury them, and you will get a new chance at life while recognizing the lives that have gone before you.

Day of the Dead Party Food

Pan de Muerto

Makes 1 loaf

5 cups flour
1/2 cup sugar
1 teaspoon salt
1 tablespoon anise seed
2 packets dry yeast
1/2 cup milk
1/2 cup water
1/2 cup butter
4 eggs
confectioners' sugar

1. Mix 1/2 cup of the flour with the sugar, salt, anise, and yeast in a large bowl.
2. In a small pan, warm the milk, water, and butter. Add the liquid mixture to the dry mixture.
3. Mix in the eggs, making sure to beat them thoroughly, then add 1 1/2 cups of the flour. Gradually add the rest of the flour.
4. Knead the dough on a floured board for 9 to 10 minutes.

Put the dough in a greased bowl and allow it to rise until it has doubled in size (about an hour and a half at sea level).

5. Punch the dough down and reshape it into a round loaf, making some bone shapes on top for decoration. Let it rise another hour. During that time, preheat the oven to 350 degrees F (175 degrees C).

6. Bake the *pan de muerto* for about 40 minutes. After baking, sprinkle it with confectioners' sugar.

Mexican Hot Chocolate with Vanilla and Chile

The grainy texture of Mexican Hot Chocolate comes from toasted ground cocoa beans, granulated sugar, and cinnamon. The intensity of the chocolate flavor depends on how much chocolate you include.

Makes 2 servings

3 ounces Mexican chocolate such as Ibarra or Abuelita
1 whole dried ancho chile
2 cups whole milk or water (see note)
1/2 vanilla bean

1. Grate the chocolate finely. Toast the chile in a small skillet over medium heat, turning it once, until it is fragrant, about 2 minutes per side.

2. Gently simmer the milk or water over medium heat in a 1-quart saucepan, then add the chile and vanilla bean. Remove the pan from the heat and steep for 10 to 15 minutes.

3. Remove the chile and vanilla bean and bring the milk or water back up to a simmer over medium heat.

4. Add the grated chocolate. Keep stirring until it has dissolved and then pour the mixture into a pitcher. Froth it with a *molinillo* (a Mexican whisk) or a regular whisk and serve.

Note: Hot chocolate made with water is lighter but highlights the pure flavor of the chocolate. Hot chocolate made with milk is creamier.

One More Creative Interlude from the Bard

Corn Husk Doll

Corn is native to North America and was sacred to the Native Americans. Besides being used for food, it has many other purposes. It can be made into alternative fuel for cars or biodegradable plastic and packing material. The husks can be compressed into briquettes for long-burning charcoal.

Native Americans gave corn as a gift to the first settlers and showed them how to grow it. Here are directions on how to make a doll that pays tribute to the spirit of the original Americans. You will need several large ears of corn and thread or embroidery floss. The soft white layers closest to the ear are the best part of the corn husk to use for this project.

DOLL HEAD

1. To make the inside of the doll's head and the beginning of the body, place two husks together, with the stiff ends in the same direction. Fold a long, soft husk into a lengthwise strip and wind it around the stiff ends to cover and secure them.

2. Choose a soft, wide husk and fold it over the top of the wound

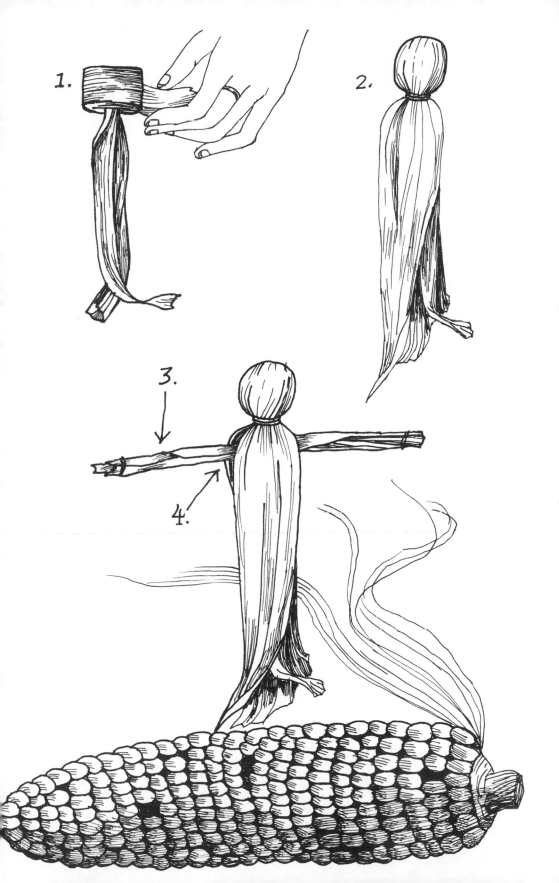

1.

2.

3.

4.

husk, making sure it is even on both sides. Wind thread or embroidery floss just under the wound husk around the neck, and tie a tight knot. This will be the doll's head.

ARMS

3. To make arms, fold two husks together and tie them in the center with thread or embroidery floss. Twist them, and then tie them at either end to make hands.

4. Split the husks in the doll body below the neck to make a slot; insert the newly made arms.

BODY

5. To form the body, fold several layers of husks over the shoulders while holding the arms in place. These will extend down the front and the back of your doll. Pick the prettiest husk to be the one on the top, then wrap and tie the waist with thread or floss.

LEGS

6. Divide the husks below the waist into two legs and wrap them in a crisscross pattern with thread or floss. When you are finished, tie the ends and trim the husks at the feet, making them even.

CLOTHES

7. Take a long, soft, even corn husk, and fold it in half. Trim it so that the edges will fall at the knees of your doll and cut a hole in the center for the head to go through. Cut fringe at the bottom. Place the garment over the doll and tie it at the waist with thread or floss.

5.

6.

7.

8.

9.

DETAILS AND FEATURES

8. The eyes, nose, and mouth can be drawn on with ink. To make a feather headdress, use a strip of husk and stick feathers into it at intervals down the length of the husk. Or cut feathers out of multicolored construction paper. For the hair, take a length of corn silk (which is under the corn husks on the cob) and fold it in half over the doll's head. Place the headdress over the hair and secure it all by sticking a thorn or a pin through both into the head.

9. If a rose bush is handy, make a peace pipe. Use a twig for the pipe stem and stick a thorn in the end for the bowl of the pipe. The mouth of the doll can be made into a hole that the pipe fits into.

Spotlight on a
Native American Hot Witch

SACAGAWEA (NORTHWESTERN U.S., CIRCA 1788–1812)

The mission of the Lewis and Clark expedition was to find a transcontinental route to the Pacific Ocean. Sacagawea, a sixteen-year-old Shoshone mother, led the group through what is now the northwestern United States, but which at the time was territory recently gained through the Louisiana Purchase. Her survival skills and serenity under pressure saved the expedition's books and instruments when the boat tipped over. She also prepared food and medicinal herbs, took care of the ill, mended clothes, and communicated with and protected the group from other Indian tribes, all while caring for her own six-week-old baby. Sacagawea did as much for the expedition as any of the men, if not more.

Seer

A Seer (also known as a Sybil or an Oracle) uses her extraordinary moral and spiritual insight to predict things to come. Using magical techniques to practice divination, Seers can find information and see the future.

✳✳✦ Crystal Ball Gazing ✦✳✳

Deciphering the images seen in a crystal ball is known as scrying. With practice, you can become skilled in this art.

Traditionally, crystal balls have been made from real crystal, like beryl or quartz, but these are rare and expensive. It is easier and cheaper to find one that is made of glass. As long as it is as flawless as possible, it is acceptable to use.

Ensure that your crystal ball is always safe and never gets scratched. Use only fine linen to wash and dry it, then polish it with a chamois cloth.

Ideally, store the crystal ball in its own room, which should be kept at an even temperature. This room should be clean, dark, and uncluttered, free of furniture except for a table for the crystal and the chairs at the table.

The optimum time to read the crystal ball is during the waxing of the moon (when the moon is getting fuller). The best lighting is diffuse natural light, which is why twilight, or the gloaming, is the best time of day. This is also called "the magic hour."

When you are ready to scry, place the crystal on a black velvet cloth to keep away reflections. No one but the gazer is allowed to touch the crystal.

Light two black candles and place one on either side of the ball. They are black so that your crystal ball will capture only the light and not the color of the candles.

Ground yourself by removing your shoes and placing your feet squarely next to each other. Sit with your back straight and focus on your breathing as you inhale and exhale. If distracting thoughts come into your mind, mentally place them in a bubble and pop it as you focus on the ball. Then spend a few moments charging the crystal with strength by waving your right hand over it. Afterward, pass your left hand over it a similar number of times to empower it with sensitivity. Repeat this until you are clear and concentrated.

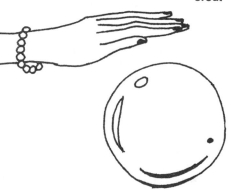

Gaze without staring into the crystal ball. Eventually, the crystal will become hazy. In the next stage, you will see clouds form in the crystal. Watch intently, as these clouds may solidify into an image.

- Clouds of white, or clouds rising upward, signify "yes," in answer to a question.
- Black clouds falling downward mean "no."
- Black clouds dissipating into lightness show that problems will be banished and replaced with joy.
- Spring green, lavender, or sky blue clouds signify happiness.
- Red or yellow clouds warn of danger. Sickness or even death is near.
- Clouds moving to the right signify a spirit regarding the gazer.

To ask about a specific person, envision him or her as you gaze into the ball.

The images you may see can be interpreted differently, depending on whether they appear on the right or left side of the crystal ball. The left signifies real things; the right shows only symbols of things. For instance, a glass of champagne on the left means there will be an actual party. But when it appears on the right, it means there will be cause for jubilation.

Crystal ball gazing is a form of self-hypnosis. You have to learn to be objective to read the symbols properly and not distort the images with your own hopes and fears. Frightening yourself with images you take too literally will not help your practice. Your gazing ability will become sharper as you learn the roadmap to the subconscious.

When clouds drift to the left, they indicate that the scrying session should end.

✦✧✦ Tarot Card Reading ✦✧✦

Tarot cards were originally used for playing games, but have served as a tool for divination for hundreds of years. There are many different ways to perform readings with tarot cards, and there are many different types of decks, with lots of beautiful and amazing artwork. But you don't even need fancy cards for the tarot; a simple deck of playing cards will still do the trick. I share the basics of this method here, and if you are interested in learning more, there are resources in the back of this book to help you.

Tarot Reading with Playing Cards

To perform a simple-spread tarot reading for yourself using playing cards, first find a quiet place where you can sit calmly and focus your mind. Hold the deck of cards in your hands and shuffle them as you concentrate on your question. Draw three cards from the deck and lay them faceup in the order that you drew them. The first card will represent the past (this can be as recent as yesterday, depending on your interpretation and your question), the second card will represent the present, and the third card will represent the future.

Simple three card Spread

```
┌─────────┐      ┌─────────┐      ┌─────────┐
│         │      │         │      │         │
│    1    │      │    2    │      │    3    │
│         │      │         │      │         │
└─────────┘      └─────────┘      └─────────┘
```

1 = past
2 = present
3 = future

Meanings of the Cards, By Suit

Hearts

Ace of Hearts: fondness, alliance, passion

King of Hearts: a young man with light-colored hair, hasty, but kind and giving

Queen of Hearts: a blond or light-haired young woman, honest and good

Jack of Hearts: a young person with light-colored hair who is a trustworthy friend

Ten of Hearts: luck, joviality, and pleasure

Nine of Hearts: a wish come true

Eight of Hearts: a crossroads, an invitation from someone (though this same card can mean a split or breakup as well)

Seven of Hearts: someone who is flighty and impetuous

Six of Hearts: benevolence from another, sudden good luck

Five of Hearts: envy, uncertainty

Four of Hearts: a possible journey, a shift, or a delay

Three of Hearts: a warning to be careful

Two of Hearts: harmony and solidarity with another

Spades

Ace of Spades: trouble, a broken relationship

King of Spades: a successful older man

Queen of Spades: a dark-haired older woman, a temptress

Jack of Spades: a kind, young, dark-haired man

Ten of Spades: fretfulness

Nine of Spades: postponements and fights

Eight of Spades: roadblocks and letdowns

Seven of Spades: possible loss of a friend

Six of Spades: hard work without reward

Five of Spades: delay, worry

Four of Spades: difficulties in work, envy

Three of Spades: disloyalty and splits

Two of Spades: backstabbing

Diamonds

Ace of Diamonds: wealth, a ring

King of Diamonds: an obstinate, forceful, light-haired older man

Queen of Diamonds: a blond or light-haired older woman, whimsical, coquettish, refined, and worldly

Jack of Diamonds: an unreliable younger-brother type

Ten of Diamonds: a trip or voyage bringing opulence and abundance

Nine of Diamonds: unexpected success in business

Eight of Diamonds: new love for an older couple, a surprise of money

Seven of Diamonds: a present

Six of Diamonds: a sign of renewed alliance

Five of Diamonds: fruitful business conferences

Four of Diamonds: an inheritance

Three of Diamonds: family quarrels or legal battles

Two of Diamonds: attachment and love

Clubs

Ace of Clubs: accomplishments, happy home life, love

King of Clubs: a sweet, dark young man, genuine and upfront

Queen of Clubs: a magnetic, willful, beautiful, dark-haired young woman

Jack of Clubs: an honest, trustworthy friend who is there for you

Ten of Clubs: surprise good luck, wealth, or a present

Nine of Clubs: new love

Eight of Clubs: wild impulsiveness, fights

Seven of Clubs: a chance for success, but the threat of a romantic rival

Six of Clubs: wealth through work

Five of Clubs: aid from a loved one

Four of Clubs: a sour turn of events

Three of Clubs: happy marriage or bond with another

Two of Clubs: sadness, estrangement

A note on the Joker: You may choose whether or not to include a Joker in your deck. If you do, and you draw this card in your reading, it indicates that you should expect the unexpected.

✦✦✦ Palm Reading ✦✦✦

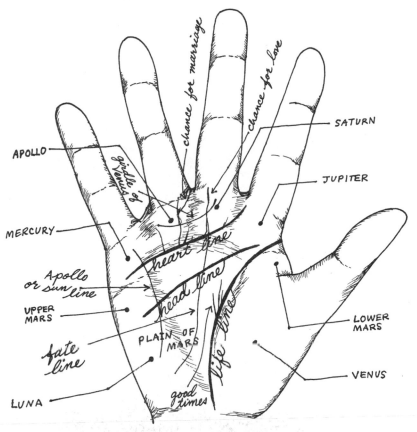

I began palm reading at the age of nine, when I received a book
for my birthday from my aunt. It was called *Cheiro's Language of
the Hand* and was first published in 1894. It opened a whole new
world for me and had some incredible photographic hand-
prints in the back of the famed actress Sarah Bernhardt, author
Mark Twain, a one-day-old baby, a suicide, and many more. It
is amazing to be able to read Sarah Bernhardt's palm over a
century later. I've included a drawing of it on page 150 for
you to practice on. May you get as much use and insight from
this skill in your life as I have.

Palm reading will give you an idea of a person's whole life at a glance. You can see how long they may live, how many chances for love they will have, how successful they will be, how they deal with conflict, how their health is, if they will marry, how they think, what their talents are, how many children they will have, if they are an old soul, if they are a leader or a follower, and much more!

Which Hand to Read

Begin with the hand the person uses most. If the person you are reading is right-handed, also consult the left hand to reveal more in the love life department, because this is the hand that is closest to the heart.

What the Appearance of the Hands Can Reveal

* Big hands are good at doing intricate, small things. Small hands like to take on and manage big projects.

* Smooth hands tell of a sympathetic nature and artistic temperament.

* Naturally coarse skin (not rough from manual labor) indicates the person is healthy, sturdy, and not easily offended.

* Thin hands show a multifaceted, flexible nature.

- Thick hands show a headstrong and willful type.

- Hands with a narrow bone structure are quick to react, but may ultimately be uncertain.

- Pale hands show a thoughtful, self-examining nature.

- Pink hands indicate a people person with a big heart.

- Bright red palms tell that the person has a hot temper.

Fingers

Length of the fingers is determined by comparison to the size of the palm. Fingers that are longer than the palm are considered long. Those shorter than the palm are considered short. People with long fingers love details. They sweat the small stuff and dress with meticulous style, though they tend to worry over trifles. Those with short fingers are impulsive and perhaps too hasty. They do not concern themselves with convention and tend to be casual in dress, quick of mind, and outspoken.

When the fingers are held together tightly and raised toward a light, the cracks and spaces between them will be revealed. These show how much money runs through the person's fingers. A person with no cracks or gaps is good at saving and budgeting. Someone with many gaps is bad at being thrifty and handling finances.

Fingers curved inward show a shy or reserved type. This person does not like to take risks. Bendy, flexible fingers denote a charming, friendly, curious person.

On the opposite side of the fingertip from the nail, you may see a small fleshy pad, shaped almost like a drop of water, in the center of the fingerprint. These are called empathy drops, which show the person is extremely sensitive and dreads causing pain to others.

Puffiness at the base of the fingers shows the person thinks only of consuming food, drink, and the like and is obsessed with comfort above everything and everyone else in life. Fingers that are very thin at the base show a fastidious person, one who doesn't eat much, drink heavily, or buy much.

Have the person spread the fingers as wide as possible while you focus on the first three fingers. If the space is wider between the first (or pointer) and second fingers, it indicates independence of thought. When the space between the second and third fingers is wider, it indicates independence of action.

The First (Pointer or Index) Finger

This is the finger of Jupiter and shows how the person relates to others and performs as a leader. When this finger is alike in size to the Apollo or ring finger, this indicates a well-rounded person who gets along with others. A Jupiter finger that is longer shows a dominant personality with strong leadership abilities. A short index finger shows someone may be inconsiderate or lacking in self-confidence.

The Second (or Middle) Finger

The Saturn finger shows inhibitions and setbacks, but also how the person deals with them and makes lemons into lemonade. An average Saturn finger, one that is about half a knuckle longer than both the first and ring finger, shows a healthy approach to life. A strong middle finger shows a strong libido. An exceptionally long Saturn finger shows someone with great strengths and abilities, but who may take on too many of the burdens of the world. This person can also act too quickly and be rash. A short Saturn finger shows an unconventional person, who may lack problem-solving skills and initiative.

The Third (or Ring) Finger

The Apollo or sun finger reigns over the arts. The typical third finger is as long as the first finger. A third finger a little longer than the first finger signifies an optimist, and one who will raise her position in life. A ring finger shorter than the first finger, however, denotes a person with a pessimistic tendency. A long Apollo finger means this person has a lot of potential for artistic talent. If the finger is very long, the drive of the person to create art will be more extreme.

The Fourth (or Pinkie) Finger

This is the Mercury finger. The tip of the pinkie typically stops at the line marking the top knuckle of the ring finger. A longer Mercury finger shows a person with a lot of self-confidence, one who will make good money. A shorter Mercury finger shows a person with low self-confidence, who may have a hard time finding a job. The extremely long Mercury finger indicates a person who manipulates through intellect, but has the capacity to make a lot of money. If the pinkie leans inward toward the ring finger, it shows someone who is good at saving money. This is also a person who will succeed on the business side of art and would make a good PR person, gallerist, or agent.

The Thumb

The thumb reveals aspects of the will and the mind. A flexible thumb indicates a flexible will that can be bent. A fixed thumb, which does not bend much, shows a strong-willed person. When the thumb is folded against the hand and the top of it stops near the inside of the first knuckle of the first finger, this is a thumb placed high on the hand. If lower, it is placed low on the hand. Too highly placed and the strong ego of this person may cause her to be selfish. A thumb placed very low on the hand can indicate someone whose mind is too easily controlled. A short-thumbed person has a hard time accomplishing what she wants to do, but she can overcome this tendency with hard work. A long or broad thumb belongs to someone who is very ambitious.

Some General Insights into the Lines of the Palm

The ideal lines are clear, defined, straight, and rosy. Pale lines indicate poor health and lack of energy and decision. Rosy lines show optimism and an active person with great health. Yellow lines reveal that the person is self-obsessed and haughty. A chained line shows indecision and the need for stability. Wavy lines weaken the power of the line.

When the entire hand is covered with a net of little lines, crisscrossed all over the hand aimlessly in all directions, it indicates the person has a tendency to worry and be anxious.

However, it can also indicate an old soul. This type of person has to learn how to be at peace.

Dots on the head line show chronic headaches, and crosses indicate head injuries. An island shows a time of crisis. Bars signify a break, such as taking a break from college or work. Squares mean a time when the person is protected from strife.

People can avoid the disasters or bad tendencies depicted on their lines. Knowing your inclination gives you the power to change it.

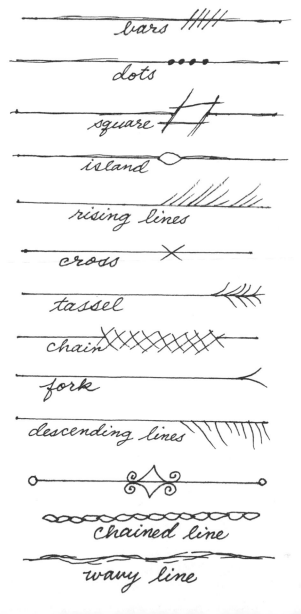

Witch Signs and Lines

A mole on the palm of the primary hand is the sign of a magical and naturally psychic person. A mole on the secondary hand shows the capacity for these talents, which can be developed with practice.

When three lines create a triangle on the palm, it is called a magic triptych. The lines that make up the triangle indicate the areas in which the person's magic is strongest.

Primary Lines

Read the palms of both hands to see the full story. For example, having a weak life line on the minor hand and a strong one on the dominant hand shows that the person has, through discipline, formed a stronger knowledge of who she is, and her health has increased. A stronger life line on the minor hand shows the person lacks ambition and may suffer from waning health due to bad habits.

THE LIFE LINE

When reading the life line, begin at the top, which is just above where the thumb is attached to the hand. From there the life line runs to all the way down toward the wrist. The life line and head line usually start together. If they split early, it can mean the person experienced an early separation from family. If the line runs all the way to the wrist or wraps around the thumb, the person will most likely live to be a hundred!

The qualities of the line determine many things. When a line breaks in the middle, then starts again, this signifies a rebirth and

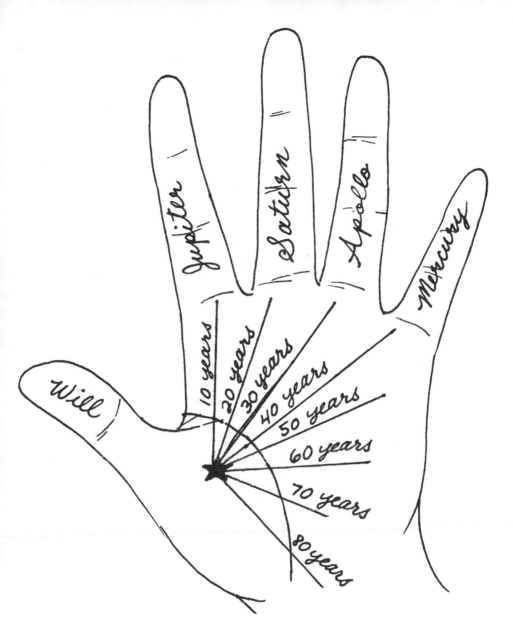

a whole new way of being. A faint or pale life line suggests health problems. It can also mean the person lives in a fantasy world and is not really present. A rosy life line etched strongly into the palm tells of robust health.

A sister line following alongside the life line adds strength to the line and also indicates the person's connection to a past life or an awareness of her destiny. This can provide aid in times of trouble.

Lines that branch up from the life line indicate aptitudes. Whichever finger the upward branch points toward indicates the skill and talent that the person has. More than one line says the person has many skills. A branch aiming at Jupiter indicates aspiration and drive that will lead to success. A branch pointing toward Apollo shows good luck and abundance. A branch to Saturn means a strong will. A branch to Mercury means business smarts.

THE HEAD LINE

This line begins beneath the mount of Jupiter and often starts by touching the life line or somewhere close to it. A deep head line shows an inclination toward intellectual stimulation and knowledge. A break can show a spotty history of education. If the headline curves downward, it signifies an elaborate fantasy life. A straight head line indicates a reality-based mentality. If the head and heart line are joined, this means the person has no separation between thinking and feeling.

The head line indicates the person's passions. Upward-reaching branches show an inclination and yearning for the qualities represented by the finger the branch is aiming toward. For instance, Jupiter equals community, Saturn equals spirituality, Apollo equals art, and Mercury means money through communication. A split at the end of a branch means the person can multitask and is able to work in two careers or focus on two interests at once.

THE HEART LINE

The heart line starts above the head line and should be read from there, running toward the first finger (beginning at Mercury and running toward Jupiter). A strong, clear, long heart line means the person is emotionally well balanced, loyal, and gives freely from the heart, expecting the same in return. A strong, deep heart line also shows the person has a healthy heart.

If the heart line ends near Saturn instead of under Jupiter, this person has the tendency to be too submissive. A heart line rising between the two fingers indicates someone who can be possessive and jealous. When the line ends under Saturn, this person has a cool, emotionless demeanor, which may stem from self-obsession or from the fear of having her heart broken. However, once the ice is cracked, this type of person can prove to be very kind, fully committing to the one she loves.

An upward-curving heart line means the person will be open about expressing love. A straight line means she will withhold emotion. A line that angles downward shows a mean temperament and tends to belong to someone who looks down on others. A fork at the end of the heart line signifies that the person must choose between lovers at some point.

Branches stemming up from the heart line signify chances for love and good relationships. Downward branches denote a failed relationship or a broken heart. A vixen who likes to flirt has many short branches going up, especially at the beginning of her heart line.

A line running up from the heart line to the ring finger signifies marriage. Lines that go toward the ring finger, but not all the way, are serious relationships that do not end in marriage.

Secondary Lines

These lines fill in the blanks left by the primary lines and help you see the whole picture.

THE FATE/DESTINY LINE

This line, found in the center of the palm, shows a person's capacity to find success in work, education, and other pursuits. The absence of this line can indicate a person who drops out of society's normal patterns.

A long fate line shows drive early in life. Energy and decisiveness are indicated by a line that continues far up on the hand. A fate line that ends at the head line can mean a lack of drive and application. Ending at the love line indicates that emotional involvements and relationships obstruct ambition. A wavering line shows a person with a faltering sense of purpose.

THE SUN LINE

Running parallel to the fate line, beneath the ring finger, this line shows the amount of innate ability combined with accomplishment. A pronounced deep line shows success and talent, along with the aptitude to manifest them. A break in the line shows a shift on the career path. The presence of more than one line or continuing branches shows multiple interests.

If there is no sun line, this does not indicate a failure; this may be a person who finds satisfaction in nonworldly accomplishments.

GIRDLE OF VENUS

This line does not appear in everyone, but those who have it are very sensual and prone to passionate romantic displays. They may provoke extreme reactions in others. A broken line shows a conflict between satisfaction and desire. A fainter girdle of Venus indicates the person has these tendencies, but they are bridled by rationality.

CHILDREN LINES

How many children the person will have is indicated by making a fist and reading how many smaller lines appear between the creases where the pinkie meets the hand and the love line.

A strong, deep line indicates a child born to the individual. A line with a fork indicates twins. Smaller, fainter lines show children who are significant in the person's life (perhaps indicating children to whom they are a mentor, teacher, aunt, or fairy godmother), but not born to them. These lines can also mean an adopted child or a stepchild. Very faint or small lines indicate children who might have been.

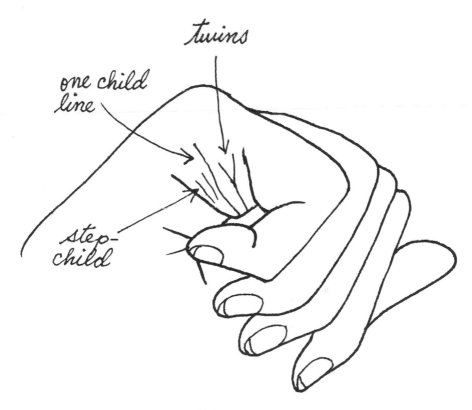

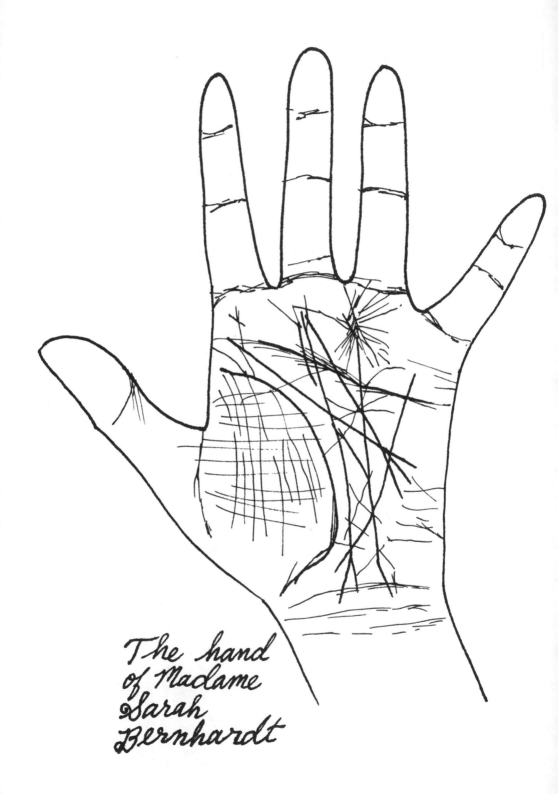

The hand
of Madame
Sarah
Bernhardt

MADAME SARAH BERNHARDT

✧ Tea Leaf Reading ✧

Brew a pot of loose tea. After steeping, pour it through a strainer. Some leaves of the tea will still come through into the cup. After the tea has been drunk, the leaves left at the bottom of the cup will form shapes. Gaze at these and interpret the shapes as one would do with clouds in the sky. Using the dream symbols dictionary that follows, you can divine the meaning of the tea leaves.

Tea leaves forming a wolf and a tree

Tea leaves forming an ocean sunset and a rainbow

Dame Darcy

✦✧✦ Dream Symbols Dictionary ✧✦✧

My favorite form of divination is dreams. Dreams are powerful and uncontrollable.

In dream interpretation, the same symbol can have different meanings. This is when you need to use your intuition. Your own experiences may tint how you perceive a symbol, so take this into account as well. All the symbols form pieces of a puzzle that you put together to tell the story that is your divination.

Airplane: a new start, a journey

Anchor: stability, something weighing you down

Apples: many children

Arrow: parties and fun, sending a letter you will regret

Baby: joy, responsibility, crying, frustration

Balloon: frustration

Basement: repressed memories

Bath: vitality, long life

Battle: conflict

Bells: joy and fulfillment

Birds: transformation from one state to another

Birth: a new beginning

Bridge: obstacles conquered

Broom: cleaning time

Bull: stubbornness

Candle flame: constancy

Castle: big goals

Cat: independence

Cave: a retreat

Circle: perfection, completion, infinity

Clock: opportunity passed

Cornfield: wealth

Crystal: matter and spirit united

Curtains: something hidden, decoration

Dog: loyalty, laziness

Door (closed): obstacle

Door (open): new chances

Doves: love

Dragon: resistance to change

Drums: family problems

Eating: boredom, craving new ideas or experiences

Fairy: fantasy

Falling: reality that does not live up to expectations

Fan: competition, a fight

Feathers (black): loss

Fire: abundance of energy, anger, purification

Flowers: contentment, pleasure, productiveness

Flying: freedom

Glass (clear): success in the future

Hammer: victory

Hands (tied): being stuck in a difficult situation

Horse: strength

Hounds: positive fortune

House: yourself

Ivy: friends, allies

Jail: inhibitions

Jumping: success

Key: solution, secret

Kiss: completion, satisfaction

Ladder: bettering oneself

Lamb: peace

Laughing: plans manifesting

Leaf: change

Light: faith

Lion: powerful friends and connections

Lizard: transformation

Lock: frustration, protection, security

Mask: deception and concealment

Mirror: falsehood, disappointment

Moon: emotion

Mother: comfort, safety

Mouse: meddling

Needle: family faults

Nest: a new home

Oak: steady growth

Ocean: healing, resolve, opportunity, spirituality

Owl: wisdom, messenger

Pirate: deceit

Police: authority problems

Pyramid: the pursuit of knowledge

Rabbit: magic, luck

Rainbow: abundant joy, transcendence

Rat: strong hidden enemies

Ring: completion, loyalty

River: spirituality, a barrier to cross

Ruins: failed plans

Running: a good journey

Scissors: mistrust

Sleeping: a time to wait

Snake: spiritual wisdom, transcendence

Snakebite: infusion of wisdom

Snow: unknown factors

Soldiers: force

Stars: hopes

Sunrise: growing awareness

Sunset: the need to protect yourself and your ideas

Swan: beauty, satisfaction

Sword: cutting through, conflicts

Teeth (aching): approaching sickness

Thief: fear

Thread: entanglements

Tree: life, psychic power

Tunnel: fear, hiding

Umbrella (closed): unnecessary worries

Umbrella (open): shelter

Veil: insecurity

Volcano: powerful feelings, passion

Wall: obstacles

Water: spirituality, emotion

Window: a clear view

Witch/Wizard: supernatural abilities

Wolf: security, insight

Zoo: confusion

✦✧ Other Signs and Symbols ✧✦

Augury

Augury is a form of divination you practice by observing the elements and animals of the natural world. Serendipity plays a large role in this game. Every cloud, flower, tree, bird, and stick can be a sign! There are special kinds of augury that use the signs and symbols of the winds, the air and sky, animals, and more. Here I will give you a glimpse of how to interpret your observations of birds and their feathers, which have strong associations with divination.

BIRDS

· A high-flying bird is a great omen.

· A low-flying bird with an irregular wing pattern is bad.

· A bluebird in spring means joy will soon come.

· A red bird foretells the arrival of a guest.

· If a robin is seen pecking at a window, a baby will be conceived by the residents of the home.

· An owl hooting three times is a warning.

· When you see a raven before a battle, it signifies victory.

THE MEANING OF FEATHERS FOUND

Brown: peak fitness

Red: superb luck

Orange: joy and pleasure

Yellow: a warning to beware of false friends

Green: adventure

James Davey

Blue: love

Purple: an exciting voyage

Black: ill portent, sometimes even death

Gray: amity and union

Brown and white: bliss

Black and white: bad luck avoided

Black and green: fame and fortune

Black and blue: new love

Gray and white: your wish will be granted

Numerology: How to Find Your Lucky Magic Numbers

Count the number of letters in your name. The number of letters in your first name is your first magic number. The number of letters in your last name is your second magic number. Add both together (keep adding until you reach a single digit), and this is the final magic number for your name. For example: Dame = 4, Darcy = 5, and 4 + 5 = 9, so 9 is my magic number.

Now add up all the numbers in your birthday, including all four numbers of your birth year. Add them until you get a final single-digit number. For example, if your birthday is June 16, 1997, you would add 6 + 1 + 6 + 1 + 9 + 9 + 7 = 39, then add 3 + 9 = 12, then add 1 + 2 = 3. This is your magic birthday number.

Add the number from your birthday and the number from your name for your final magic number. Keep adding until you reach a single digit.

✦✧✦ The Seer's Witch Holidays ✦✧✦

Seers are excellent at illuminating the darkness, so it makes sense
that they love the celebrations of the darkest time of the year.

Yule (or Midwinter Solstice)

This pagan midwinter festival, which takes place around December 21, was eventually absorbed by the Christian celebration of Christmas, and many of its traditions were adopted. Decorated pine trees (symbolizing everlasting life), the Yule log, wreaths, gift giving, costumes and plays, caroling, wassail, holly, and mistletoe were all originally parts of the pagan celebration.

In the Northern Hemisphere, this time of year brings the longest night, and the return of light to the earth, which has been cause for celebration throughout human history. It is a very important time of year, when the sun god is said to be born from the womb of night. In ancient Rome, this night was deemed *Dies Natalis Solis Invicti*, which translates to "Birthday of the Unconquered Sun."

Candlemas (or Imbolc)

This holiday falls on February 2, midway between the winter solstice and the spring equinox. It is the festival of waxing light, for the sun is now making its path into the lighter side of life. To celebrate, torches and candles are lit to blaze through the darkness of this cold month.

This holiday is also called Brigid's Day, for the Irish goddess of inspiration, fire, healing, poetry, and midwifery. One of the rituals for Brigid is to make a little doll in her image, then make her a doll bed and put her to sleep.

Have a Saint Brigid crafting day by the fire with your friends. Make the little doll and bed, or any other knitting, sewing, drawing, or craft project that appeals to you. Drink herbal tea to celebrate her healing powers and give each other hand, foot, or shoulder massages.

Before going to bed, take a nice long bath with lavender bath salts. (Combine 2 cups Epsom salts and 1 cup dried lavender in a big bowl, stir well, and pour into a jar.)

More for All Hot Witches

This last section is for all types of witches. Here you can read about your astrological sign and how to be a street-smart witch. You can also learn about hot witches from the past, how to form your own coven, where to find ingredients for the activities in this handbook, and more awesome books about things that interest you!

Astrology: The Twelve Signs of the Zodiac and What They Mean

There is more to astrology than the horoscopes printed in the daily newspaper. If you are interested, you can learn a lot by mapping your astrology chart and finding out about your rising sign, moon, and planets, in addition to the sun sign under which you were born. There are reading suggestions in the back of this book for those who would like to explore astrology further, but the sun signs are a good place to start. You may have heard the recent hubbub about the earth's position affecting the constellations and therefore the signs of the zodiac. But astrologers do not believe that the shift in the earth's position over time makes a difference in the way the zodiac is used in astrology. So here are the signs, along with their classic dates.

ARIES

March 21–April 19

You are a fire sign, and your favorite color is probably red. Your planet is Mars, which sometimes makes you feel like a Martian, but along with this comes the special power of perception only Martians have. You are a good leader and have a young, charismatic spirit.

TAURUS

April 20 ~ May 20

As an earth sign, you are a grounded and loyal friend. The way you like to think and live is by careful, logical steps, one at a time. You are a great cook and make a house a home. But if you get mad, everyone will know about it!

May 21–June 20

As an air sign and the sign of the twins, you are two of a kind! Talking all the time, you flit from one party to the next on your colorful fairy wings. Great at multitasking and making friends, the unstoppable Gemini can do anything (except make up her mind).

CANCER

June 21–July 22

A sensitive, poetic water sign, you gaze at the moon and wander by night. Like a crab, you sidestep any trouble. Sometimes you just need to hide in your shell and arrange all your feelings because, like the ocean, your emotions are so deep.

July 23–August 22

Vivacious Leo, your golden life is lived in the sun (or spotlight),
and your fiery personality makes you a number one candidate
for rock star in any profession. Winning friends along the way,
you roar to conquer any situation.

VIRGO

August 23–September 22

Thoughtful, considerate Virgo, you pay great attention to every detail. "Make new friends but keep the old; one is silver and the other gold" is your motto. You are intellectual and an earth sign, so if something is not logical, you dismiss it.

LIBRA

September 23—October 22

A real people pleaser, your goal is to make everything fair. You are good at solving other people's problems. However, you are constantly trying to keep in balance. You give very good advice, but seldom follow it yourself.

Gctober 23—November 21

You are a water sign with the passion of a fire sign. You will protect your true friends through any weather, but if someone turns on you in even the slightest way . . . STING! You are full of secrets, and the way you keep them to yourself makes you even more fascinating to others.

SAGITTARIUS

November 22–December 21

You are fun and fiery, centaur! You're always up for travel and adventure, and you love to party with the friends you make everywhere you go. You are adept at many things and passionate in your beliefs.

CAPRICORN

December 22–January 19

Although you are an earth sign, you are so grounded you are more of a solid-rock sign. You like logic and routine, but you also have a special charisma (like fellow Capricorns Elvis, Dolly Parton, or Martin Luther King, Jr.). Family is important to you. And you can see the light through any dark situation because your life started in the darkest days of the year.

AQUARIUS

January 20—February 18

Magic Aquarius, as a water bearer, you think you must be a water sign, but you are much more complex than first impressions reveal—you are really an air sign. You have the ability to transform yourself, as if by magic, much like the condensation of water from the air, which eventually will rain back down again as water.

February 19 – March 20

Dreamy Pisces, you are the true hopeless (but hopeful) romantic. You can and will make all your dreams come true if you can only find your other shoe! Oh, well, what does a fish need with a shoe anyway?

Cusp Babies

If you were born on the first or last day of a sun sign, this is called a cusp. Cusp babies will probably benefit from reading both their own sun sign and the sign that ends or begins right before or after their date of birth. For example, if your birth date is December 22, your sun sign is Capricorn, but you probably have some Sagittarian traits as well.

✨✦ Tips for a Street-Smart Witch ✦✨

What Smart Girls Know

First and foremost, always trust your instincts. Have your radar on. Anyone who is conscious of her energy can do this. Think about when you are at a fun party, how your energy goes out and you shine. Now think about when you are reading a book or standing and observing, how your energy is self-contained and you can draw it into yourself. Practice this to make yourself invisible.

The Cloak of Invisibility

When you go out at night, go ahead, wear a fancy hairdo. Or wear it down long. Wear a cute, sexy, sparkling dress. But make sure to bring a dark-colored coat or long black cloak with a hood or even a sweatshirt hoodie. Covering your hair makes you less noticeable. Turn yourself into a shadow with your dark coat; this is your "cloak of invisibility." You can see but not be seen. The light does not bounce off you, but is absorbed by you and into nothingness. Keeping a low profile on the street at night will help you avoid unwanted attention. When you get to the party and you're with friends, you can throw off the cloak and let yourself shine.

Protective Magic: Iron for Women

Iron in our diets makes our blood strong, and iron objects protect women from evil of all kinds. Iron will make you more vital and energized, and it can make your magic powers stronger, so you are better able to protect yourself.

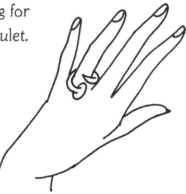

- Bend a used horseshoe nail into a ring for an extra-strength luck/protection amulet.

- Wear clothing with iron nails sewn into the hem.

- Your hand will have reinforced magical and protection power when you wear an iron bracelet.

- For protection while you sleep, slip a horseshoe under your pillow or keep a fireplace poker under your bed.

- Sleeping in a bed with an iron frame is like sailing a boat of safety on a sea of dreams—it enhances health and creativity while you sleep.

Herbal Protection for Home and Person

Collect white handkerchiefs and pale blue ribbons or thread. In the center of the handkerchiefs, place a handful of St. John's wort, dillweed, and vervain. Create sachets by tying them closed with the ribbon or thread. Hang them throughout the home and wear one around your neck or stash it in your purse.

Keep-Out Powder

Crush a red brick into powder and sprinkle it in an unbroken line over all entryways to the house. Spirits or people with evil intent will not be able to cross the line.

✦⋆ Hot Witches from Herstory ✦⋆

Here are some goddesses and historical women who were definitely hot witches! We learn a lot about famous men, but there have been amazing, powerful women throughout history. They were influential, creative, and always themselves. Look up more awesome women in the sources listed in the back of this handbook or find them all around you among your family and friends.

PRIMORDIAL GODDESS (BEGINNING OF TIME)

In ancient times, people knew so little about how babies were made that they thought women would just swell up for no reason and one day another human would burst out of them. For this reason, the Primordial Goddess was regarded as the primary creative force of the universe. People believed that the world was made by this female god who either conceived alone or with a male whom she had also given birth to. She was the source of everything, and everything returned and was related to her. Plants grew from the earth the way babies sprang from the body of a woman, so earth, life, and the feminine were all connected.

GODDESS HECATE (ANCIENT GREECE)

Goddess of the crossroads, Hecate embodies three phases of womanhood—maiden, mother, and crone—in one. Hecate is one of the most ancient Greek goddesses. She is an important goddess to address and understand, because in understanding her, we accept, own, and nurture even the dark sides of ourselves. Hecate also shows us how to accept and honor ourselves in all phases of life: when we are young, middle-aged, and elderly.

If you are confused about which direction to go in your life, or want to take a new path and make a great shift, Hecate will aid you if she is properly addressed. Witches gather to worship her at crossroads on the eve of a full moon. An altar is placed there, and offerings of food and wine are left. The one who leaves the offering walks away and does not turn back, because to catch a glimpse of Hecate is a sacrilege. Hecate can also be called on during the dark of the moon to banish old negative thoughts and feelings or to render justice and bring new positivity.

Hecate has three sacred symbols: a key to the underworld, with which she unlocks the secrets of life after death and the occult mysteries; a rope, symbolizing the umbilical cord of rebirth and renewal; and a dagger, or athame, a symbol of ritual power.

SNAKE GODDESS (ANCIENT CRETE)

The snake goddess was the basis for the mermaid. She is depicted as half woman, half snake (which looks something like a mermaid tail), and also as a mermaid with a snake. Just as a woman goes through ever-changing cycles (maiden, mother, crone, as well as the cycles of her monthly period), the snake goddess transforms as well, changing her skin.

All sea goddesses reflect the sea's qualities. The sea can be gentle and nurturing or violent and deadly. Just as it is alternately beautiful, cruel, tender, loving, calm, or destructive, so too can mermaids and other sea goddesses be.

When a woman of any age is drawn to the image and idea of a mermaid, what she is really doing is getting in touch with the goddess.

VALKYRIES (NORSE MYTHOLOGY)

Valkyries sat high in the sky with thick, long blond braids, eagle wings, and metal hats lined with fur and topped with huge horns. The clouds were their box seat as they watched mortals battle below. When warriors died, the Valkyries chose which ones to take to Valhalla, a hall of the dead watched over by the Norse god Odin.

AMAZONS (ANCIENT GREECE)

The Amazons are featured in Greek history, mythology, and visual art. They flourished on a lost island off the coast of North Africa and in another society on the coast of the Black Sea. A predominantly female society, they were self-sufficient and renowned martial artists and athletes. They were said to be tall, beautiful, and strong. They did not need the company of men except when meeting up to procreate in springtime.

HILDEGARDE OF BINGEN (1098–1179, GERMANY)

Hildegarde of Bingen spent most of her life in a convent. After receiving basic training from Anchoress Jutta, Hildegarde took over her position as abbess. She became the leader of a little congregation of women who took an interest in her. Mystical instructions told her to relocate her convent to western Germany and settle near the town of Bingen, but powerful men of the Church tried to cut her funding and claimed her revelatory visions were false—they allowed her to go only after she became very sick.

In Hildegarde's cloister, she was regarded as a powerful and prestigious figure in politics and religion. Her studies and drawings are noted in the most ancient, meaningful metaphysical manuscripts of the Middle Ages. Her manuscripts profiled her divine visions and their enlightening meanings. She composed music and wrote prominent observations on the Scriptures and the Holy Trinity, claiming that strong faith was the keystone of a moral and spiritual life. Cataloging countless medicinal plants, she had extensive knowledge of drugs and herbs and was renowned for her cures. Despite her strong religious nature, she was the first woman to properly describe female orgasm.

But the greatest accomplishments of Hildegarde of Bingen were her musings on the relationship between humans and the Universe as Divine. Taking a holistic approach, she claimed no separation between the spiritual and the psychical. Hildegard described her vision of the universe as a cosmic egg.

cosmic egg

CHENG I SAO (EARLY 1800s, SOUTH CHINA SEA)

The pirate queen Cheng I Sao was known as Shih Yang until she married the pirate captain Cheng I. It was a long-standing tradition in southern China for women to work alongside men on freighters, passenger boats, traders, fishing junks, and pirate ships. Families lived their entire lives at sea. The average sailor lived in an area about four feet square, shared by his wife and any subsequent children.

But Cheng I Sao had more power than most of the seafaring women—or men. Together, she and her husband worked to make the rest of the pirates in the area their allies. By 1804, their collaboration had resulted in a unified force; seven major pirate captains signed their constitution, and over four hundred junks and seventy thousand men enrolled in the renegade navy. In 1807, when Cheng I died, Cheng I Sao became the commander in chief, the pirate queen of them all.

Through brazen piracy, ransoming prisoners, and an enormous, lawless protection scheme, she made a fortune. If the community in question did not pay her fees, her confederates would burn and plunder the town, enslaving all in their wake. After each dark victory, the pirates celebrated, gambling and smoking opium.

MARIE LAVEAU (AROUND 1794–1881, NEW ORLEANS, LOUISIANA)

The daughter of a socially elite French-American and his black mistress, Marie Laveau could play both sides of the fence. She helped the poor people of her community, but she also worked as a hairdresser and stylist to the rich. She was adept in medicine and magic as well. She held voodoo ritual/rock shows attended by people from all races and economic classes, where she danced with a snake to the accompaniment of drumbeats. The events provided newly arrived slaves with a place to dance and stay in touch with their African traditions. At the same time, curious rich whites begged Marie to allow them to attend. They also hired her to create gris-gris (little bags filled with herbs and spells) for them, thereby integrating ancient voodoo with contemporary Catholicism.

There are many legends about Marie. It was said that she gave birth to fifteen girls through only five pregnancies, thus creating her own family coven. My theory is that she had such control over her body and mind (like a Sufi monk) that when she became pregnant she split her fertilized egg into multiple embryos. When yellow fever hit her area, many people died, but Marie put a protection spell of salt around her home, and all her family members were spared.

Marie remained so youthful that when her daughters grew to womanhood, no one could tell her and her daughters apart. There is a story that a slave was being unjustly hanged in the town square and Marie did not approve, so her coven arrived at the scene, a group of identically tall, beautiful women with their hair tied up in African scarves. No one could tell which one was the original Marie. As the time for the hanging drew nearer, a violent thunderstorm arose over the platform. All who were gathered quickly dispersed due to the foul weather; the condemned man was lost in the chaos.

When her girls grew up, she trained the eldest, named Marie after her, to do her job. As the mother Marie grew older, the daughter Marie took over and kept the family tradition alive. Mother Marie lived to be nearly ninety years old, which was an astounding feat in her time. Her tomb can be seen in New Orleans, where she lived most of her life, and there are still many descendants of Marie Laveau in New Orleans today.

How to Create a Coven with Your Own Sister Witches

Here is an example of a way to start your own local coven to bring you and your friends closer together. A coven can give ladies of all ages a place to gather and have people they can turn to. It can be started anywhere: just get a group of friendly girls together and set up a meeting time. You can have anything you want on your agenda; this is one way to get you started.

1. Dress up and bring something special to eat or drink: this is a celebration! Observers who do not want to perform the group's rituals are allowed. Nothing negative is permitted in the coven's circle, only positive affirmations and support.

   No one has to do anything she doesn't want to do; the ideas that follow are merely guidelines to help you connect to yourself, to your friends, and to women from the past. Guys are allowed, if you want, but this should also be a place of female power.

2. Sit in a circle and introduce yourselves. Feel free to own the term "hot witch" by inserting it in your name as a title, nickname, or what have you. For example, Dame "Hot Witch" Darcy or "Hot Witch" Isabelle.

3. After you have said your name, celebrate a positive thing that you did or accomplished today. Even if you are having an otherwise bad day, there is always something positive. It can range from "I baked brownies, and they turned out terrific" to "I passed my English test" to "I got to sleep in today."

4. Friends in the circle congratulate, et cetera, and then the circle moves to the next person for her introduction and announcement of what she wants to celebrate.

5. After the introductions, everyone gets a large piece of paper and a small piece of paper. On the large paper, write your hopes, dreams, and desires. You will take this home and post it on your bedroom door or anywhere prominent, where you will see and remember it.

On the small paper, write one wish. This will be the one you are hoping to manifest with the power of yourself and your friends. Fold it, write your name on it, and put it in a box.

6. One person leads the ritual. Read something about a hot witch from history. This will require some preparation. I recommend consulting any of Judy Chicago's works. She published an amazing book called *The Dinner Party*, which profiles thousands of women, from the primordial goddess to relatively modern Americans. Or look up goddesses, patron saints, or historical figures on your own.

7. Perform a ritual relating to the chosen hot witch. Chant, drink special things, dance—anything you want! The leader of the ritual shows the others what the ritual is about. It doesn't have to be long or elaborate, just heartfelt.

8. When the ritual is done, sit in the circle and spin a bottle. The person the bottle points to will lead the next ritual. If she doesn't want to, spin again until it lands on someone willing.

9. If you want, and everyone is comfortable with it, hold a prayer for the dead. An example:

This prayer is for all the witches of the past who were burned and killed or fought for women's rights. We remember them and honor them now. May they rest in peace.

Name the witch from history you are celebrating today. Other coven members can add names of loved ones who have passed on. You can look up other prayers for the dead—Egyptian, Latin, Buddhist, anything you want—and use these prayers, too.

10. Decide where and when the next meeting will be and what you will celebrate and do. This is a good time for questions or comments.

11. Have fun! That's what this is really all about. Have a tea party, a dance party, a knitting party, or just hang out with your hot witch friends!

✧✦✧✦ Hot Witch Friends ✦✧✦✧

My Hot Witch Friends

Sometimes it seems like there's no one out there who thinks that being weird and different is great. But actually there are so many amazing hot witches out there—I've been lucky enough to meet a lot of them! In these pages, I've highlighted some of my hot witch friends. These women are grown up, doing creative, interesting things, and are just fine being their weird selves.

Jessie Evans
Musician, Performer,
Producer
Berlin, Germany

Mara Haseltine
Submolecular Sculptor,
Underwater Eco-Artist, Professor
New York City

Angela Devine
Mother, Stitch Witch, Clothing
Designer, Founder of Guthrie Lane,
Cowgirl, Believer in True Love
Livingston, Montana

Miss KK
Costume Designer, Stylist,
Fashion Consultant
Los Angeles, California

Rachel Amodeo
Photographer, Rock Drummer,
Actor, Screenwriter, Producer
New York City

Jessica Delfino

Guitar, Ukulele, and Rape Whistle
Player; Singer of Songs about
Unicorns, Rainbows, and Vaginas
New York City

Kai Altair

Songstress, Dancer, Dreamer
New York City

Ophelia DeLaFuente

Artist, Belly Dancer
Savannah, Georgia

Shien Lee

Event Producer and Stylist, for
Dances of Vice
New York City

Batcakes

Puppet Maker, Circus Performer/Fire
Eater, Stunt Woman, Writer, Hat and
Accessory Designer, Owner Fashion
Company Batcakes Couture
Los Angeles, California

Miss Renee, aka Tarot Chick

Empath, Tarot Card Reader,
Spiritual Astrologer
Portland, Oregon, and
Seattle, Washington

Trina Robbins

Writer, Herstorian, Pagan
San Francisco, California

Your Hot Witch Friends

Here's some space for YOU to paste pictures of hot witch friends, family, and women you admire. Don't forget to put in a photo of yourself!

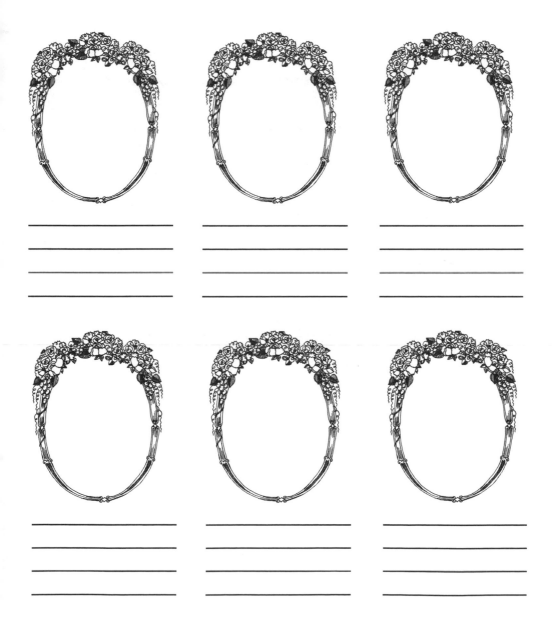

✦✧† Where to Buy Ingredients †✦✧

All the spells and activities in this book can be completed with items easily found in your local grocery or arts and crafts store. Many of the herbs listed can be bought in the spice section and in the tea section. For instance, to obtain edible lavender and hibiscus, just get the tea.

You can also check out your local health food store or look online. There are stores that carry ingredients for making candles (for example, thecandlemakersstore.com or GloryBee.com), or for making soap (GoPlanetEarth.com, SoapMakingStore.com), and there are loads of general arts and crafts stores (Michaels, Jo-Ann Fabric and Craft Stores, Hobby Lobby). You don't need special equipment or expensive items, though, for the activities in this book—with simple, common ingredients, you can be on your way to magic!

✦✧† More Reading †✦✧

Want to find out more about palm reading? Drawn to meditating? Craving fairy tales or raw food recipes or doll-making projects? There are plenty of books out there with information and activities and stories on whatever interests you. Here's a list with some of my favorites to get you started.

Al-Rawi, Rosina-Fawzia, and Monique Arav (translator). *Grandmother's Secrets: The Ancient Rituals and Healing Power of Belly Dancing.* Northampton, MA: Interlink Books, 2003.

Barrett, Francis. *The Magus: A Complete System of Occult Philosophy.* York Beach, ME: Red Wheel/Weiser, 2000 [originally published 1801].

Beard, Lina, and Adelia Beard. *The American Girls Handy Book: How to Amuse Yourself and Others.* New York: BN Publishing, 2009 [originally published 1887].

Cheiro. *Cheiro's Language of the Hand.* Teddington, Middlesex, UK: Wildhern Press, 2007 [originally published 1894].

Costello, Patrick. *The How and the Tao of Old Time Banjo.* Crisfield, MD: Pick-Ware Publications, 2003.

Eisler, Riane. *The Chalice and the Blade: Our History, Our Future.* New York: HarperCollins, 1987.

Goldschneider, Gary, and Joost Elffers. *The Secret Language of Birthdays.* New York: Penguin, 1994.

Illes, Judika. *Encyclopedia of 5,000 Spells: The Ultimate Reference Book for the Magical Arts.* New York: HarperCollins, 2009.

Kemp, Gillian. *The Fortune-Telling Book: Reading Crystal Balls, Tea Leaves, Playing Cards, and Everyday Omens of Love and Luck.* Boston: Little, Brown and Company, 2000.

Laurel, Alicia Bay. *Living on the Earth: Celebrations, Storm Warnings, Formulas, Recipes, Rumors, and Country Dances Harvested.* New York: Random House, 1971.

Louis, Anthony. *Tarot Plain and Simple.* Saint Paul, MN: Llewellyn Publications, 1996.

McElwee, Meg. *Sew Liberated: 20 Stylish Projects for the Modern Sewist.* Loveland, CO: Interweave Press, 2009.

Roche, Lorin. *Meditation Made Easy.* New York: HarperCollins, 1998.

Schauffler, Grace L. *How to Make Your Own Dolls for Pleasure and Profit.* Whitefish, MT: Kessinger Publishing, 2008.

Stroller, Debbie. *Stitch 'n Bitch: A Knitter's Handbook.* New York: Workman Publishing Company, 2003.

Tatar, Maria (editor). *The Classic Fairy Tales.* New York: W. W. Norton & Company, 1999.

Tourles, Stephanie. *Organic Body Care Recipes: 175 Homemade Herbal Formulas for Glowing Skin and a Vibrant Self.* North Adams, MA: Storey Publishing, 2007.

Tudor, Tasha. *A Time to Keep: The Tasha Tudor Book of Holidays.* New York: Simon & Schuster, 1996 [originally published 1977].

✦ Acknowledgments ✦

Thank you to my agent, Jane Lahr, and to Maya Gottfried, my dear friend. Also to Kate Farrell and Rebecca Hahn at Holt; your advice and guidance polished this project into a clear and beautiful jewel. And to the dedicated and loyal team, Vincent D. Dominion, Philip DeWolff, Tony Boies, Melanie Bentley, Skippy Spiral, Eric Wiler, Kyle Hoover, and everyone at Under the Rainbow in Savannah.

This book is dedicated to my lovely and magical mother, Lila Ann Wickham, forever a true flower child, feminist, crafter, and nurturer. As someone who worked in the nursing profession your whole life, you know the secret of true nourishment (so much so that my brothers are six foot four!). You fed our growing spirits and bodies, so that our every cell was filled with light and with the vegetables from your fairy garden. Thank you for the gift of radiant health and eternal happiness; it's a blessing knowing you

Baby DD and Mom

are always there for us, like the Mother Goddess herself. I respect your work ethic, and I appreciate how I could always ask you any questions—on topics ranging from medical issues to spirituality to relationships—and get a straight, honest, and educated opinion in your own voice. I'm happy you have now become the amazing artist I always knew you were.

Grown-up DD and Mom

This book is also dedicated to my six Fairy-Godchildren, two of whom are pictured. Atticus is the oldest; he is thirteen and is an animator and silk-screened clothing designer, and he makes his own comics, dolls, music, and more. Tasja is also thirteen. She is a wonderful photographer and draws amazing mermaids and fancy ladies (which are all really self-portraits). She told me once when she was little never to step on

Art Star of NYC
Atticus Jones

mushrooms because fairies live there. Also, this book is for Bella, Odin, Luther, and Cosimo and his brother Jasper.

Thank you to my lovely interns and art students who have graced my life in past, present, and future. You are the inspiration for this book and have taught me so much. My family and friends, witch and mermaid sisters (which are all the same thing), your support means the world and all other worlds to me. Witch sisters: Niki Smith, Mara G. Haseltine and Pat Gercik (her mom), Satanica Batcakes, Blake and Peter Olmstead-Mavrogeorgis, Jessica Delfino, Rachel Amodeo, Seze Devres, Nora Keyes, Kristine Karnaky, Meg Mack, Mimi Mayer, Natalie Ribbons, Justine Brown, Kai Altair, Bambi the Mermaid, Adriana Iris Boatwright, Miss Oblivious, Renee Dunn, Ruqayyah Preister, Elena Kanagy-Loux, Brandi Obsolete, Jessy Champagne, Amber DeCelle, Dawn

DD and Tasja doll crafting

Garcia, Chantel Richardson, Natalie Valentine, Natalie Behring, Alix Sloan, Kelly Kuvo, Angeliska Polacheck, Johanna Spoerri, Lisa Crystal Carver, Blair Barnette, Lisa Hammer, Kate Hambrecht, Carissa Neff, Madeline Von Forrester, Carolyn Turgeon, Deborah Czersko, Veronica Varlow, Go Go Max Bernardi, Gala Verdugo, Whitney Ward, Maxx McKenzie, Gala Darling, Molly Crabapple, Poptart Sprinkle, Heathervescent, Anitra Opera Diva, Beth VanTosh, Ophelia DeLaFuente, Leah Zipkin, Jackie Hernandez, Dawn Sharp, Tamaryn, Jennifer Ballestas, Whitney Matheson, Nancy Jones, and everyone in the EZ Bake Coven. And the ladies of my family: Great Grandma Edith Marler (your cowgirl memory lives on forever in me), Grandma Edith Stanger, Grandma Mel, Linda and Alexa Stanger, Kim and Emily Kwamme, and Angela and Guthrie Rose Devine.

And last but not least, this book is dedicated to all the girls and ladies of the world, and to you, dear reader, for magic and fate have drawn this guide into your hands. We are fairies, so there is no death.

Dame Darcy

Dame Darcy currently resides in New York City and Savannah, Georgia. She is known worldwide as an illustrator, writer, fine artist, musician, filmmaker, animator, environmentalist, and Cabaret Mermaid. Her illustrated titles include *Gasoline*, *The Illustrated Jane Eyre*, and *Frightful Fairytales*, and she has been publishing her comic book series, *Meat Cake*, for twenty years. She's also the lead singer in the band Death by Doll. She is the creator of an online forum for girls called the EZ Bake Coven and an online game based on *Meat Cake* called Paper Doll Dreams.

damedarcy.com